- How I beat heart disease and the FDA.

- Head-off your heart attack with herbs.

- Lower cholesterol & blood pressure naturally.

- The "12 Day Flush" cleans your arteries.

- Herbs for safe energy every day.

- Heart herbs that can save your life!

- Herbal cures for everyday ailments.

- Dangers of heart Surgery, and Drugs.

- New ideas for a happy, healthier life without drugs or surgery.

*The Chinese word for crisis is
"dangerous opportunity."*

LEFT FOR DEAD

by Dick Quinn

Contributing Writers
Shannon Quinn &
Colin Quinn

Cover Design by Traver and Assoc.
Herb Illustrations by Kathy Vaneps
& Karen Berry Flemming
Typography by JEZAC Type & Design

Special thanks to
George Town
friend and poet

LEFT FOR DEAD

R.F. Quinn Publishing Co.
Box 17100
Minneapolis, MN 55417
(800) 283-3998

Dedicated to Elsie Madison,
the lady at the lake.

CONTENTS

MY STORY

by Dick Quinn

"The individual has the right of his own wisdom to choose methods for his well being and longevity. This right is not to be taken from us."

—Arthur L. Kraslow, M.D.

My Credentials

I am an expert on heart disease because I have it. I have had a heart attack with a near death experience, an angiogram, a double coronary bypass, heart failure and an incredible recovery. An herb I discovered has kept me alive and given me excellent health, vigor and energy since October 21, 1978.

There is no question what was wrong with me. I had severely blocked arteries which the doctors said required surgery. I can show you the scars. After surgery, my energy, vitality and general health declined rapidly. My condition deterioriated for six months. I fainted often, experienced dizziness and sudden loss of energy. Finally, I had a long, frightening blind spell one afternoon. In spite of the cardiologist's continued reassurances, I knew I was dying. Then I discovered the herb that made me well.

Today, I am very much alive. I don't need heart or blood pressure drugs, so I'm not impotent or constipated and don't have kidney or liver failure. I'm not depressed. I am energetic, ambitious and enthusiastic. I feel good every day.

The herb I discovered works so well for me, I want you to know about it. I discovered other herbs you should know about, too. Maybe they will work for you, as they have for me.

1
HOW IT STARTED

It was May, 1978. I was 42 years old, wrote magazine stories and ads for a living and felt fine. I only weighed a few pounds more than I did in high school and had quit smoking a year before. My wife, five children and I lived on a farm in Wisconsin.

My blood pressure had been high since I was 16; it ran in the family. So did strokes and heart attacks. My mother survived a heart attack at 38. My father and his brother both died from strokes at age 47. Their sister also died of a stroke. All four of my grandparents died before I was born. Everyone in the family had circulation problems, but I thought I was in pretty good shape.

One night, I came home from work to discover our 1,500 pound family steer in the neighbor's field eating corn stubble.

It was a chilly evening. I walked across the pasture and began to chase him home. Suddenly, I had an unusual and very unpleasant pain in both arms. It felt like the veins and arteries on the inside of my arms collapsed. It took several minutes for the pain to stop. I suspected the pain was angina, but hoped it wasn't. Angina would mean heart trouble. Big trouble for me. I was only 42. I wasn't supposed to have a heart attack yet.

The next night, I went outside briefly and the pain happened again. It seemed the chill brought it on. I called the doctor.

The doctor examined me and monitored my heart with an electro-cardiogram. The next day, I returned with my tennis shoes to take a stress cardiogram. I ran on the track until I collapsed. The doctor then announced he thought he had found a "problem."

I think the "problem" was actually a heart attack I had during the stress test. The doctor scheduled me to enter St. Mary's Hospital in Minneapolis the following Tuesday to have an angiogram. He gave me a bottle of nitroglycerine tablets with solemn admonitions to "stay home, don't get excited, don't work—just rest and take two of these every four hours until you check into the hospital on Tuesday for the angiogram."

I could not believe this was happening to me. I tried to relax over the weekend, but didn't get much rest. I couldn't seem to recover from the exhaustion I felt from the stress test. I had an early appointment Monday morning with a new client.

My heart attack

I got up at 6 a.m. that Monday to drive the 35 miles to St. Paul. It was May 29, 1978.

I felt terrible all during the drive. I was sick, shaky, sweaty and very tired. I stopped at a diner to buy coffee and a roll. I hoped the caffeine and sugar would make me feel better. They didn't.

At 8:00 a.m., I was waiting for an elevator in a Minneapolis office building, on my way to the meeting. I felt terribly sick and tired. It had taken real effort to carry my briefcase up the steps and into the building from the car.

It was an expensive new black glass building with an atrium soaring over the lobby. I put my briefcase on the floor and stood waiting for the elevator. I remember looking straight ahead and just standing there, trying to rest standing up, like a horse.

Suddenly, an overwhelming presence seemed to take charge of my spirit, my life force, my soul, my being. By whatever name, my life was in its hands. I was swept up irresistibly with incredible power.

It seemed my spirit was being separated from my body, so my body could die. I was connected to my body by only the most tenuous thread. Soon, that part of me would die. My body would be discarded, worn out. There was no pain. I wasn't tired anymore. I felt comfortable, peaceful and strangely powerful.

I soared high above, leaving my body standing before the elevator. I was suddenly floating in the air, watching myself down below.

My body didn't collapse or fall in pain, it just stood there. I felt an almost physical link or connection with my body. The connection could break at any moment. I couldn't control it, but I could wish. I could hang on, perhaps wish my soul back into my body. I tried hard not to let go.

I met my mother, who had died months before. I saw her as a hazy light among a group of lights I recognized as her friends. I knew her at once. Her aura was her unmistakable signature.

"Oh, there's Dick," I heard her say. "We're over here, Dick." I wanted to join her. It was so inviting to just let go of life, become a light and live forever.

There were other people with her, other lights. I recognized them as people I knew who had died. They had no bodies, but I knew them. I recognized their spirits.

I didn't see God. I had no forboding. No feeling of impending judgement, punishment or retribution, but rather a welcoming.

My death experience was very pleasant and peaceful. I realized death is nothing to fear.

Death is not ominous or threatening unless you're an evil, hurtful person. I think evil people meet their victims when they die.

I discovered it's most important in life to be kind. I realized many of my major concerns are utterly trivial and silly.

The people I met didn't urge me to join them, but they couldn't give me life, either. They just let me know I was welcome. "Join us any time," they seemed to say. I remembered my Dad and the day he died. I was 9 years old. It is the most momentous event of my life and the saddest. I will never forget a second of that terrible day. I thought of my youngest son — he was 9 years old. And my other children. They would be so hurt, so shocked and saddened, like I was. I didn't want to do that to them. I felt I could only want to live. I couldn't make it happen, but if I wanted to live badly enough, maybe I would.

I wished for life as hard as I possibly could. I concentrated on living. I held on tight and strained to get back into my body and finally it happened.

I returned to my body and felt peace. I was stunned into contemplative silence for a while. I just stood there, by the elevator, in that big, black glass building in Minneapolis. The entire experience took only a few seconds; had it taken longer, I would have died.

I had seen death and lived.

My heart attack happened when the blood flow to my heart was blocked for a few seconds by an obstruction in my left main coronary artery. My heart misfired like a water pump sucking air. That's what happens in most heart attacks. It's sudden, inexorable, utterly overpowering. You are a passenger on the life and death train. You can't stop it and you can't get off. You wait to see if you live or die.

There was no pain. It didn't hurt at all. I just drifted into the most fantastic experience of my life.

In some ways, the kind of heart attack I had is the best and worst kind. The left main coronary artery is the most important of all. When it gets blocked, the heart attack doesn't hurt and the trip is incredible, but you usually die. There's only a 30% chance of survival and then maybe as a mushroom.

I lived, but one day I will die. It could happen any time. Death will be an entirely pleasant state, but I want to postpone it as long as I can. There are a lot of lovely things you have to be alive to do.

I returned to my body and lived on that day in May 1978. I was at peace and no longer felt ill.

Life goes on. I rode up several floors on the elevator, stopped at the men's room to wash my face and went to the meeting. Then I went home.

That was the day I died for the first time.

THE
Heart Foods Story

Nearly dead following heart attack and bypass surgery, this powerful "heart food" gave me energy and vitality that's lasted 10 years. It gives me strength to enjoy life every day and a wonderful feeling of well-being without harmful drugs.

GUARANTEE

I guarantee the quality, purity and potency of safe, natural "50/50" Power Caps.

The original "Power Caps" label.

Power Up! Feel Good Fast!

Herbal Energy Formula

"50/50" POWER CAPS

Safe, Natural, No Caffeine.

♥ Heart Foods, Box 16324, Mpls. MN 55416

THE
Heart Foods Story

Nearly dead following heart attack and bypass surgery, a "heart food" I discovered gave me energy and vitality that's lasted 10 years. My "brain food" has more of the 2 most powerful brain herbs. It gives me thinking power, confidence and a more positive attitude.

GUARANTEE

I guarantee the quality, purity and potency of safe, natural "442" Thinking Caps.

Heads Up! Feel Good Fast!

Herbal Brain Food

"442" THINKING CAPS

Safe, Natural, No Caffeine.

♥ Heart Foods, Box 16324, Mpls. MN 55416

The original "Thinking Caps" label.

"Physicians pour drugs of which they know little, to cure diseases of which they know less, into humans of which they know nothing."

Francois Voltaire (1694-1778)

2

THE MEDICAL PROCEDURE

My angiogram.

The next day I had an angiogram at St. Mary's Hospital in Minneapolis. The cardiologist ran a wire through the artery in my arm to my heart. He examined the arteries and heart chambers with a little television camera and measured the blood flow. We could both see the problem.

The left main artery to the heart was 98% blocked. He said it provided the blood that powered the heart muscle itself. If the artery closed for even a few seconds and shut off the blood flow, I would have a heart attack with only a 30% chance of survival. I knew all about it. I had that heart attack the day before, but I didn't tell him about it.

I agreed to have emergency bypass surgery, because I expected to die at any time without it. I had absolutely no fear of death and felt at ease now that I thought my family knew what to expect. It was O.K. to die now. I needn't feel guilty about hurting my children, as I had been hurt years before. They were ready for it now.

Life or death — let it happen.

My bypass.

The next morning, they washed me down with hair remover, knocked me out, put me in a trough of ice water, put tubes in my mouth, nose, penis, stomach, wrist and lungs, and took me to the operating room.

The surgeon cut me open, then split my breastbone with a bone saw, pried my chest apart and opened the sack enclosing my heart. He put a tube from the heart-lung machine into my heart's right atrium to remove the blood from my body and another tube into the aorta to return it, bypassing my heart. The machine oxygenated my blood enough to keep me alive and pumped it through my body.

Meanwhile, another surgeon was opening my right leg from ankle to knee to remove the saphenous vein, used for the bypass.

They stopped my heart with a muscle-paralyzing potassium solution, cut openings for the two bypasses and sewed pieces of my leg vein in place. They re-started my heart with an electric shock, put it back inside my chest, clamped my chest shut with two stainless steel hog rings, sewed up the 13 inch long opening and delivered me to Intensive Care.

A bunch of us were cut that morning, assembly line style. Truly a remarkable performance by remarkably skilled people working together like a precision drill team, in an extraordinarily equipped operating theatre at a cost of many dollars and much pain. Too bad it doesn't help the patient.

It was June 1, 1978, two days after my heart attack.

I awoke in Intensive Care a few hours after surgery, filled with tubes, terribly thirsty and uncomfortable, trussed up like a Thanksgiving turkey. I wasn't in pain; the drugs took care of that. The operation had been a massive intrusion into my body. Not a heart attack, but an attack on my heart.

I was completely at ease when I faced surgery because I had no fear of death. I wanted to live, but I wasn't worried about it. I knew life or death was beyond my power to control, so I'd just go along and see what happened. I think being relaxed helped me suffer less soreness from the surgery.

I regained my strength quickly after surgery and got out of Intensive Care in record time. Since I had no fear prior to surgery, I was relaxed and suffered little physical trauma. Others in the Intensive Care unit hurt a lot more than I did and seemed to recover more slowly. The smokers were especially miserable because it was harder for them to breathe and it hurt so much to cough.

Within days, I was discharged from the hospital, a star patient.

My decline.

I began to feel myself getting weaker almost the day I got home. I tried to take long walks, as the physical therapist at the hospital advised, but I felt faint at the least exertion.

After I had been home about a week, I decided to drive to a nearby lake for some sun. It was an eventful decision.

I met an acquaintance at the lake, an older woman who was the mother of a friend. She noticed I was exhausted after the short walk from the car to the lake shore and abruptly told me to begin taking Cayenne Red Pepper right away. I lay on the sandy beach under some young willow trees, utterly spent. She spoke of Dr. John Christopher and said Cayenne would help me recover my health and prevent another heart attack.

It seemed preposterous to recommend Red Pepper after what I'd been through. As if that could help. This was too serious for such nonsense. She told of seeing Dr. Christopher recently at a seminar in a midwestern hotel. During a break in the proceedings, a man had a heart attack in the lobby. Christopher hurriedly gave the man some water with Cayenne mixed into it and he was up and walking around in a few minutes.

I didn't believe her. A heart attack can't be that easy to deal with. The man must have had something else wrong. She must be mistaken.

I was still lying on the sand, trying to recover from the walk. "You look terrible," she said. "You need Capsicum— Cayenne Red Pepper."

She continued to talk about it, but I just tried to politely ignore her. It was absurd to think that anything as complicated and serious as heart disease could be treated with a spice from the grocery store. She couldn't possibly know what my cardiologist didn't know. He had a wall full of degrees. He knew what was best for me — that's why I put him in charge of my life. He knew everything. I had to trust him with my life, or die.

I'd never try something as crazy as red pepper without asking him and I wouldn't want to ask him. It would be embarrassing. He might feel I was questioning his ability with some weird voodoo medicine idea. He might get mad and make a fool of me. He would think I was challenging his authority, suggesting there was something he didn't know. Maybe he wouldn't like me anymore and wouldn't try as hard to save my life. He was the Angel of Death. I was to do as he said, then God might let me live. I was to obey. And if I died, it would be neat and orderly — the accepted way. It would be "God's will."

Besides, my cardiologist would make me well. "As good as new," he told me. I was sure he would. It's like a religion: you have to have faith in your doctor to be saved. Giving up faith and having your doctor desert you is more frightening than dying. Besides, I had invested all this pain and anxiety, I couldn't quit now. I had gambled so much, the doctor had to be right. Everything was riding on him.

Her words reverberated in my head: "You should take Cayenne Red Pepper," she said. But that was heresy. I tried to put it out of my mind. I couldn't bear to think she was right. After all this — all the money, all the pain, all the effort. All for nothing.

No, she couldn't be right. She's just an "herb person," leftover from the 60s. I'll show her. I'll get well, just as the doctor said I would. I'm coming along fine.

I followed all the rules when I got home from the hospital. I ate no bad fat, thought no bad thoughts, avoided stress, exertion and excitement. I went for slow walks and tried to exercise, but just got weaker.

Apparently my arteries collapsed from the stress of the surgery or became completely blocked after the bypass, decreasing the flow of blood through them. The veins they used to bypass the blocked arteries just couldn't handle the job. My heart wasn't getting enough blood. It's called coronary insufficiency. My heart was failing. It was running out of gas.

I expected to die at any moment.

I lived like a mushroom, hiding from death. Every day I got weaker. I looked and felt like I'd been hit in the chest with a bowling ball. I had no pep, no stamina, no energy, no color, no enthusiasm. I was too depressed to kill myself.

The family spoke in hushed tones when I was around. Mustn't upset poor old Dad, lest he break in half or clutch his chest and fall over dead. I had become a ghostly visitor in my own home.

I was a fragile, wimpy, stoop shouldered, impotent shadow of myself. On many occasions, I suddenly lost my energy and collapsed, like a deflating balloon.

I fell into the magazine rack at Walgreens, crushing a stack of *National Enquirers.* I fainted in the checkout line at the Target Store and at several supermarkets. There was no warning: I'd just have to sit down. NOW. It didn't matter where I was. I was afraid I might collapse when I was driving a car or walking across the street.

If I had to go to a supermarket, I would find the bulk dog food, so I could sit on the bags between forays into the food aisles. I planned every move, anticipating collapse.

It could happen at work, shopping or anywhere. I couldn't open heavy doors, lift, work or exert myself in any way without passing out. I was the family mushroom, too fragile to withstand loud noises or disturbing news. For months, I couldn't even drive a car.

One day in October 1978, six months into my "recovery," I had a blind spell. It was about 1:30 in the afternoon. I was vacuuming an upstairs bedroom, when it suddenly grew very dark. At first, I thought it was an eclipse. I looked outside, then turned on the overhead light and saw the bulb as a dull, gray glow. I realized I was losing my sight.

I felt my way downstairs without knocking any pictures off the wall and sat on the couch, wondering what to do.

I was completely blind except for a little open spot in my periphery. It was like looking at a plate glass window with brightly colored paint running down it. At first, I could see the colors — red, yellow, blue, green. Gradually, I became totally blind and could see nothing. I waited there in the darkness, wondering if my optic nerve would be destroyed, wondering if I would ever see again.

I don't know how long I sat there. It seemed like hours, but I was alone and couldn't see the clock. I thought of calling someone, but I couldn't see to dial the phone. Besides, what would I say? Hello, I'm blind. So what? There was nothing anyone could do.

It didn't hurt. There was no pain at all. No headache, no nausea. I was just blind.

I tried lying down, but nothing changed. I shook my head and rubbed my eyes, then massaged the back of my neck. Nothing. I put my feet against the wall and hung my head down toward the floor, so I was upside down. I even hit myself on the head, but nothing changed. I was still blind.

I sat on the couch for a long while and waited, wondering if I'd see again. Wondering if I would die. I had read that when the optic nerve is deprived of blood, you go blind, perhaps forever.

After a while, I lay down on the couch and waited. Slowly, slowly my sight returned.

My six month check-up

A few days after the blind spell, I saw the cardiologist for my six month check-up. It was the 20th of October 1978, a Tuesday. The six month check-up was an important benchmark after a bypass, when recovery should be complete.

I had seen my cardiologist every couple of months since the operation. In every visit, he told me I was "coming along fine," no matter how badly I was failing. At first, I wanted to believe him so much, I did. That was over now. Lying wouldn't work any more. I couldn't ignore blindness. I couldn't ignore death. I couldn't keep lying to myself.

Of course, I told him about the blind spell while he was examining me. It was the first thing I said. He ignored me; said nothing — as if I hadn't spoken. He just finished listening to my chest, told me it was time for my regular x-ray and left the room. It was as if my complaints were so trivial, they didn't deserve a response from the Angel of Death. He was above that. How dare I challenge him for an explanation. But all I wanted was hope.

After the x-ray, he came back into the examination room to tell me to make another appointment. I should have another angiogram, he said. I might need another coronary bypass.

I couldn't believe he would suggest something that already failed and left me an invalid. He must have a better idea.

I had to have an answer. I told him I was not "coming along fine," as he told me over and over. I was dying. My blindness couldn't be ignored. The answer wasn't more of the same thing that didn't work in the first place. Something had to be done now. Something new.

"What do you expect," he indignantly demanded. "They took your heart out of your chest, stopped it, cut it and sewed on it. You can't expect it to run right."

I was an ignorant, naive fool to expect to be "as good as new," just because he told me I would be. How dare I hold him to his word. He was above that. Important people like him can lie any time they want. It's almost mandatory — especially when speaking to commoners like me.

I had counted on him. I had put my life entirely in his hands. He was the expert. I expected him to have an answer, to give me hope. Instead, he got angry and rejected me. "Go die," he seemed to say. I was left for dead.

He couldn't handle failure, so it had to be my fault. I was a failure because I was dying. Failures should go away and die. I was shocked, then angry to realize he had accepted my death. I expected him to keep trying. There were few heart drugs then, thank God, so we didn't play chemical roulette. He wanted to sell another angiogram and bypass for $20,000 or $30,000. I wasn't buying any. It didn't work the first time and I was too disgusted to ever consider it again. Another bypass was unthinkable.

Surgery was easy for him to push; he didn't have to go through it, to feel the pain and helplessness. It was as easy as ringing up a sale on his cash register. Another day, another referral fee.

He had seen my death coming closer and closer with every visit to his office, but he told me I was "coming along fine," just as he told my wife and my daughter I would be "as good as new." That's how they sell the surgery; they sell the family, so the patient feels obligated to have it to allay their concerns. When he dies, "it's the will of God." Nobody need feel guilty.

At that moment in the cardiologist's office, I realized it was entirely up to me to heal myself. I knew nothing at all about treating heart disease, but I had to take charge. He was dropping me. He had done what he knew how to do and now he didn't have to care anymore. He followed the accepted procedures. They didn't work, but that was O.K. The patient should now die quietly, without making a fuss.

The doctor was exonerated. He was a dealer, not a healer. Patients die all the time; what's important is being politically correct. Modern medicine rejects the old ways and has no new ways that work for what I have. He didn't let failure lead him to try other therapies, just because they might save my life. He knew what was really important.

I had thought he wanted to save my life at any cost, but my life was only important to me. He was only interested in patients who recover. Nobody likes a loser. My cardiologist had no time for failures like me.

He walked out of the examination, leaving me to my thoughts. I felt like I had been slapped in the face. It was stunning: He had taken me this far and then dropped me.

The Angel of Death can go to hell — I'll do it myself. I'll save my own life, somehow. I don't know anything about heart disease, but I'll figure it out and take charge because I have to.

I walked out of his office that day, already thinking of the lady I had met by the lake six months before. "You need

Capsicum," she had said. "Cayenne red pepper." Now it was the only game in town.

My doctor was supposed to have the knowledge, so I thought I didn't have to understand it. He would do the thinking; I would simply obey. I was dying from heart disease, but I wasn't even sure what it was. Cayenne. It won't do any good, but it's the only thing anybody ever suggested, the only idea I had. I didn't know what to do, but I had to do something right away. I needed the hope. It didn't matter that it wouldn't work. It was incredibly lucky that I remembered her.

I drove directly to the General Store in Somerset, Wisconsin, bought a can of Fairway brand Cayenne Red Pepper for 69 cents, went home, emptied a few capsules from an old prescription, filled them with Cayenne and swallowed three. I didn't expect anything to happen and, for the moment, nothing did.

Dick Quinn mixing up some of his original "Power Caps" in his kitchen.

"...if the whole materia medica could be sunk to the bottom of the sea, it would be all the better for mankind and all the worse for the fishes."

Oliver Wendell Holmes, M.D.

3
MY RECOVERY

I have always been a late sleeper — especially after my heart trouble — but that day I woke up about an hour earlier than usual. I couldn't understand it: here I was awake earlier than usual and I felt like getting up. Usually, I awoke tired. I didn't think of the Cayenne.

I went downstairs to the kitchen, sat at the table and drank my decaffeinated coffee, while I waited for nap time, like I usually did. But that day was unusual.

I felt strangely impatient, even energetic. In fact, I felt so good I put on a coat, scarf, gloves and hat and went outside, still wondering if I were up to it. I felt terrific, but I was afraid to trust it. Maybe I'd go outside and faint.

Though it was only October 21, 1978, an early snowfall slid off the house and deposited four feet of heavy wet slush on the porch roof. I had asked my sons to shovel it off after school that night, so the roof wouldn't collapse.

I felt so good when I got outside, I carried the ladder to the porch, so they'd be sure to shovel off the porch roof. Normally, I wouldn't have carried anything as heavy as a ladder, but I didn't feel normal.

I found the shovel for them. Then I decided to put the shovel up on the roof and maybe just push a little ice off the edge, so it wouldn't break the drain or eave.

It felt so good to feel good. I climbed up on the roof and began pushing the ice off the edge. Then I started to shovel. It was heavy, wet snow four feet deep, but it seemed easy. Soon I'd shoveled off the entire porch roof, all 28 feet of it.

There was a huge pile of snow below the porch roof.

"Don't push cars, get into fist fights or shovel snow," they warned after my surgery. But I felt so good I just did it without thinking. It was entirely impulsive. I didn't realize how irrational my behavior was until I finished shoveling and jumped off the roof into the snow pile.

Suddenly, I realized what madness it was to shovel snow. Even healthy people had heart attacks shoveling snow. I took myself into the house scoldingly, like a mother with an errant child, and sat on the living room couch, wondering what had come over me. Then I remembered taking the Cayenne Red Pepper. I ran out to the kitchen and took three more capsules of Cayenne. I have taken it every day since.

It's just incredible—nothing less. I have controlled my heart disease, staved-off a heart attack, felt terrific and enjoyed a wonderful quality of life for years because of a common kitchen spice. Cayenne is my "wonder herb." I would not be alive today without it.

I have never gone back to the doctor—he has nothing for me. I have something for him, but I don't think he wants to hear about it. It's only good for the patient, not good for business.

Cayenne is an herb and herbs are not scientific, so it doesn't matter that they work. Thousands of years of clinical experience don't matter. Repeated healing successes don't matter. Saving your life is not as important as being scientific. It's better to die scientifically. Drugs are scientific, so it's O.K. to kill you with them.

You usually find out you have heart trouble when you have a heart attack. It is often announced by sudden death. You drop dead, as I nearly did in 1978, or you get a terrible pain in the chest or shoulder, can't breathe, feel an enormous weight pressing against you. You're out of control. You have no power. It's too late. You can't stop it. You just wait around to see if you live or if you die, like a spectator at a ball game. It's that close.

There is no warning. You're not given six months to live or anything so dramatic, you just die. Suddenly it's all over.

That's your lot, if you have heart trouble. But at least you can finally stop worrying about cancer. Cayenne keeps sudden death from happening to me. It is my shield. It keeps me alive—no question about it.

Every single day I bet my life on Cayenne. I put all my chips on it. I haven't had a prescription for anything since 1978. I don't take any drugs for blood pressure or fibrillation —just Cayenne and a few other herbs every day. I never ever miss a day.

"Heart Disease" isn't really a disease, it is an incurable condition that begins at birth and goes on forever. You have it as long as you live. If you are an 18 month old infant, your arterial deposits are already beginning; if you are older, the deposits are bigger. If you are an American, assume there will be a problem. Your heart is fine at first, then clogged arteries interrupt the blood supply, so you have a heart attack and heart damage. You can head off the heart attack by keeping your arteries clean, but you have to clean them every day. You can't take drugs every day because they build up and poison you or stop working. Drugs are short-term poison therapy: great if you want to kill something, but no good for healing. They aren't even good for you.

You get heart and circulatory problems from the foods you eat; you can only control them with the foods you eat. Herbs are food medicines that can help solve problems caused by other foods.

Your doctors probably don't know about herbs, because they weren't taught about them in medical school. Herbs are treated contemptuously by the American medical establishment. Arrogance justifies ignorance. Herbs are old fashioned, unscientific Third World medicines used by witch doctors.

Medical doctors in Germany, China, India and the rest of the world use herbs because they work. They want to heal the patient, even if it sells no drugs. In nearly every country except America, herbs and other "alternative" therapies are conventional.

Herbs often work better than drugs or surgery for heart disease, are usually much safer and cost the patient far less pain, risk and money. But herbs are plants and can't be patented like drugs. The drug company can't have a monopoly, so you can't have the herb. There's just no money in herbs. That's why you get drugs and the knife.

For 40 years, the FDA has tried to make herbs and vitamins prescription drugs, so drug companies can monopolize them. When that happens, you and I lose the right to take care of ourselves. We lose the right to "life," as the Constitution guarantees it.

The big drug companies are now searching the jungles for "wonder herbs," but we won't benefit until they patent the drugs, if they ever do. We must all have access to these healing plants as they are discovered. Sick people cannot wait for the FDA to guarantee drug companies monopolies, so they can extort money from the dying. We can't let greed kill us.

The medical schools, AMA politics and simple arrogance keep your doctor ignorant; the Food & Drug Administration keeps you and me ignorant.

The FDA won't let the people who sell herbs tell you how they work without "scientific" proof. Since herbs are natural, not scientific, they can never be proven scientifically to work with the double-blind studies the FDA accepts. You can never be told what natural medicines do. Keeping secrets is as simple as that. Your doctor isn't taught how herbs work, so he can't prescribe them. The FDA and drug companies don't want you to know, so they won't tell you. The herb company can't tell you.

Herbs are secret. You have to find out about them by accident, like I did, or through a book like this one. I love to tell secrets.

My experience proved to me that surgery to clear arteries and prevent heart attack doesn't work. It is nearly always a mistake. A very painful, very expensive bandaid that probably won't increase your life expectancy or prevent a heart attack. It could leave you a babbling vegetable with brain damage or other infirmity. Surgery hurts you. It helps no one but your doctor, the surgeon, the hospital and others in the money stream, who aren't worth dying for.

Better if you just give them the money on condition they don't touch you; then go home and pretend you're recovering from an operation. The rest will do you more good than anything.

Or you can have the $4,000 angioplasty, the $40,000 bypass or other fashionable procedure. Pay the money, take the risk, make your doctor happy, keep the hospital humming, put your family's concerns at rest, suffer the pain. In a little while, do it again — unless you die first.

I had a double coronary bypass about 14 years ago — four times longer than a bypass is supposed to last. The comedian Jackie Gleason had his first bypass the day I had mine. He subsequently had three more. Then he died. The poor man. He had so much money they cut him to death. According to "modern medicine," I should be dead by now, but I am very much alive, thanks entirely to "ancient medicine."

My bypass was actually a failure from the very first. It closed within a week. Herbs reopened my arteries and saved my life. I bet my life on Cayenne in 1978, and won health and energy. I won freedom from debilitating, expensive, addictive drugs and from impotence, constipation, depression and pain. I've escaped angina, headaches, leg cramps, flu, and low energy. Drugs haven't damaged my kidneys.

If I die tomorrow, that's O.K. I'm already a winner, years ahead of the game. I'll be really alive right to the end. It feels good to feel good; I remember when I didn't. It's nice that everything works. I'll take Cayenne every day until I die. It keeps me alive and lively. It's my miracle. My mean old junkyard dog that protects me from the killer. Herbs like Cayenne do it all for me.

Since I became my own physician in 1978, I've done a terrific job with an impossible patient who eats all the wrong things and breaks all the rules. A real bad actor. The credit goes to Cayenne and that lady by the lake. My eternal thanks to her.

This is not a game with me. I have a fatal condition, for sure; could pop off at any time. I've already had my preliminary interview.

I make the decisions because I'm doing the dying. I have a right to the information I need to make those decisions, but there are powerful business and government people who want to deny me that right. They don't want you to know, either. But I'll tell you.

As human beings, we deserve every chance to live, even if it's bad for the Life & Death Industry. We have that right, even if it makes drugs harder to push and drug company stocks drop a bit. The right to "life" is in the bible and the U.S. Constitution. No human being in any position has the right or authority to deny me knowledge and medicines I need for my own health. Certainly not a governmental agency like the U.S. Food and Drug Administration. God and the Constitution gave that right to me.

Thousands of years of human experience shows there are safe ways to clean your arteries, strengthen your heart and prevent heart attack. But we must take our drugs and get cut to be profitable, so that's what we get.

Our medical people should want to know about every cardiovascular therapy. They should want to know what works, what might save your life, because you or someone you love will almost certainly need it. But they don't want to know.

It would be bad for sales. Drug pushing would drop off. No more sales commissions for heart surgery; no more drug "seminars" in Hawaii. No more drug company jobs for retiring FDA employees. Herbs can prevent heart attack. I know they can. I bet my life on them and I won. They work. Am I ever glad. Your doctor should study herbs in medical school, so you can benefit, but that won't happen. It costs important people too much money to save the lives of people like you and me.

For a couple years after my operation, I got letters from the hospital asking, in effect, if I were dead yet. I answered every one with my message about Cayenne. They weren't interested. I realized then that we patients and victims must care for ourselves because the caretaking establishment doesn't care.

Healthcare should be like a buffet dinner. All the treatment options—all your choices—should be on the table. Over there we have the surgery choice, next to it drugs, then herbs, chelation, nutrition, acupuncture. Everything should be on display, so you can make an informed choice. But it isn't that way. Your right to choose is denied.

First Law, Hippocratic Oath: Primum non nocere. Above all, do no harm.

Surgery and drugs are harmful, so they should be prescribed by the doctor as the very last resort, a desperate course of action not even considered until every safe, effective therapy is tried.

Big hospitals have expensive operating theaters and high buck surgeons, so you get the knife. Many hospitals actually pay commissions to M.D.s for referrals. It's like selling used cars, but not as ethical.

Coronary bypass surgery happens in America 380,000 times every year because, it's incredibly profitable. Most patients have health insurance that pays about $40,000 per hit. With any kind of complications, the sky's the limit. It's a dream business opportunity. Everyone benefits but you, the patient. You are a very valuable piece of meat. They don't want you to go to the health store for treatment.

Herbs heal; drugs kill. But drugs are "scientific" and can be easily monopolized for incredible profit. Herbs are cheap—even free. They work. Nearly all are safe, but some herbs are dangerous. Some are even deadly. And some are miraculous. They are powerful medicine. Since American medicine banned herbs in preference to drugs in the 1930s, doctor-caused illnesses and deaths have soared. We really have become "a nation of junkies," as Dr. Robert Mendelsohn predicted in his book, *Confessions of a Medical Heretic.*

If you live in Germany, Japan, China, India—nearly anywhere—your doctor and you have safe herbal options. In Germany, you can buy dozens of different medicines made with herbs and clearly labeled for your heart; here you have to guess. In other countries you can be treated for almost anything without ruining your health, your life and your finances.

In China, your doctor is paid more if he keeps you healthy; here it's most profitable to make you sick. You and your doctor are kept ignorant of safe treatments. You're supposed to shut up and do your drugs. Get low. American doctors are taught that medicine is like war: you have to destroy the body to save it. They treat illness with poisons and knives that "do harm." There are many medical systems in the world, but none is as harmful as ours.

You and I are victims of this ignorance. Your doctor is a victim, too, because he risks losing your trust and losing you as a patient. If he finds something seriously wrong, you go away to be treated to death. We pay with our lives and money; your doctor pays for his ignorance with frustration and failure.

I hope my experience helps you

I am not a doctor or medical expert. I took charge of my own health care in 1978, because my cardiologist dropped me. Thank God he did. The only medical training I remember was when I learned artificial respiration in the Cub Scouts.

I do not advise anybody but myself, and there are times when even I don't listen. I have found many herbs that work safely for me, cost little and are easy to self-administer. I prescribe them for myself every day. I want you to know about them and other therapies I've run across, since your doctor probably doesn't know.

If you want to learn more about herbs, go to your health food store, if the FDA hasn't shut it down, and choose a book on them. There are many good books now on herbs and other safe therapies.

Holistic doctors know about safe therapies. Many chiropractors, naturopaths and herbalists know. Your own doctor should look into it. It's time you know, too. That's why I wrote this book.

4
SINCE 1978...

I'm partial to Cayenne, because it saved my life. That made quite an impression on me.

After my discovery of Cayenne in 1978, I decided to learn all I could about it and tell everyone what it has done for me. I had not yet tried any other herbs. In fact, I was still skeptical about them, but I was absolutely sold on Cayenne. I carried it with me everywhere, and still do.

I began looking for herb books. There weren't many in 1978 and some I found didn't even mention Cayenne, others didn't seem to know it was for the heart. I couldn't believe there was such ignorance about the herb that was keeping me alive and would help so many other people.

I threw away the Diazide the cardiologist had prescribed to lower my blood pressure. After I stopped taking it, my blood pressure went down. I didn't have angina anymore, either, so I threw away the nitroglycerine tablets, too. I haven't had a drug prescription since.

It was fortuitous that I stopped using the Diazide when I did. A 1991 study showed that type of diuretic actually causes heart attack, as well as chemically induced diabetes.

By 1980, I was buying Cayenne in bulk from grocery stores, buying the largest capsules I could find and filling my own. I took two or three capsules every morning and more later in the day, if I felt tired.

In 1981, I found the book *Capsicum* by Dr. John Christopher. Christopher was a genius from Utah who discovered incredible things Cayenne can do and used it as the primary ingredient in his herbal formulations. Other herbalists use low powered Cayenne, but Dr. Christopher recommended the very hot little Birdseye peppers from Africa. He was right. I had discovered the less potent Cayenne didn't work as well anymore. I had built up a tolerance.

Hot peppers are rated by heat units, just like whiskey is rated by proof. The higher the heat units, the hotter the pepper and more powerful it is as a stimulant. Cayenne for cooking ranges from 2,000 to 5,000 heat units. Jalapeno peppers and Tabasco sauce come in at 20,000 to 30,000 heat units. Most Cayenne sold in health food stores has 40,000 heat units. The African Birdseye Cayenne that Dr. Christopher recommends has 130,000 to 150,000 heat units. You can feel the difference.

The heat comes from a substance called Capsaicin, which is in all hot food. Cayenne has five different types of Capsaicin and more of each type than other peppers, so it is much more effective medicinally.

On numerous occasions, Dr. Christopher actually stopped a heart attack in progress by giving the patient Cayenne in warm water. It can also be put under the tongue if the patient is unable to swallow.

About 95% of all heart attacks occur in a coronary artery that has become narrow because of cholesterol and plaque. When you are stressed, as many people are on Monday mornings, your artery contracts, making the narrowed section even smaller. That's when a blood clot can come along and block your artery completely, shutting off the blood to your heart and causing a heart attack. Cayenne dissolves the clot, opens the artery and stimulates the heart, stopping the heart attack.

Studies conducted in Thailand show Cayenne prevents a heart attack or stroke before it happens by lowering the fibrin in your blood, so blood clots can't form.

Fibrin is a blood protein that causes clotting. Caffeine and most other stimulants cause your arteries to contract, raising blood pressure and forcing the blood through your system with more power. It's like tightening the nozzle on a garden hose. You get power, but you pay a high price in damage to your body.

Cayenne "jump starts" your heart with a shot of strengthening energy. Your arteries open wide, so your body gets the circulation it needs without straining your heart. You get energy you can feel — without damage. Cayenne doesn't raise your heartbeat or blood pressure. Unlike caffeine, Cayenne is good for you. It is nature's most powerful stimulant.

Dr. Christopher used Cayenne as his crisis herb to stop internal and external bleeding, treat shock and in other life threatening emergencies. He made a Cayenne and oil paste that grew hair when rubbed into the scalp. He put the paste on the sole of the foot to restore circulation for diabetic people threatened with amputation due to gangrene. He even used it to treat hemorrhoids and ulcers successfully.

Dr. Christopher discovered hundreds of uses for Cayenne, but its most important role involved the heart and circulation. Improved circulation is the key to better health in many ways including digestion, elimination, energy, sex, attitude, complexion, respiration, sleep, ambition, stamina, eyesight, ulcers and headaches. Cayenne improves circulation all over your body.

Like other herbs, Cayenne has a healing action that effects the whole body and has many ancillary benefits. You might take it for one problem and find it corrects another.

Nutrition is the basis for prevention of illness, and herbs are the most nutritious of all foods. They are ideal for health maintenance because you can take them every day, forever providing the nutrients your heart and other organs need, without danger of fatal overdose.

I have used herbs to stay off prescription drugs since 1978. My circulation is terrific. I am a high-energy person in excellent health. When I start to get a cold or sore throat, I take Goldenseal and Fenugreek to take care of it. When I feel tired, I take Cayenne and get good energy that doesn't hurt my heart. When I'm tense, I use Valerian to help me relax.

Herbs are foods that heal, but cannot be sold as medicines. Over 50 years ago, American medicine adopted the "scientific method." All health claims must be scientifically proven. Herbs are natural vegetables, so they vary in size, weight and potency and don't lend themselves to scientific evaluation. Nature isn't scientific. Herbs can't be standardized, like drugs.

The FDA only accepts double-blind studies where one group takes the herb, another takes a sugar pill. No one is supposed to know which one he is taking, but you can taste, smell and feel many herbs. They can't be tested that way, so we can never prove scientifically that herbs work and no "claims" can be made.

You can't consider natural alternatives if you don't know about them. If you can't get the information you need to make a choice, you are deprived of your right to choose.

If the people selling herbs tell you what they are for, the FDA threatens them with medical fraud and puts them out of business. It doesn't matter how many clinical studies show the herb works. It doesn't matter that the herb has been used safely for two or three thousand years. Experience doesn't matter. The people's needs don't matter. Your health and safety have nothing do with it. Only money matters.

The FDA is supposed to promote your health and mine by objectively assessing treatment options and telling us about them. They should scour the world, searching for the answers, then shout them from the rooftops. Instead, they hide the information I need for a long, healthy life and pretend to be protecting me.

If the FDA won't help me help myself, it should get out of the way. Stop pushing drugs. Stop censoring information about natural medicines and help all Americans live longer, happier lives. We have the right to know about all our health options; they have the obligation to help us find out.

Murder your mother

Deadly drugs should be taken off the market immediately, no matter how much money is involved.

Halcion is a sleep drug that doctors say causes blackout, memory loss and other psychiatric problems including violent behavior. It makes simple insomnia a life-threatening affliction.

Evidence Halcion causes psychotic behavior is so convincing, a jury acquitted a Utah woman of murder. She shot her mother eight times at midnight on the day before her 83rd birthday, then placed a birthday card in her hands. She had no previous history of mental disorder or violent behavior. The jury found her "incapable of voluntary action" while under the influence of Halcion.

The FDA spokesman said on NBC televison news: "There is no scientific proof Halcion caused the woman's behavior." The benefit of the doubt goes to the drug. You must prove your case scientifically. Maybe you have to murder your mother in an FDA laboratory.

Doctors reported so many psychiatric problems from Halcion, it was banned in Europe, but the FDA didn't even require a warning on the label.

Seven million Halcion prescriptions are written for Americans every year, but instead of warning us of the danger, the FDA has banned the natural sleep products that are known to be safe and effective.

More and more people are using herbs instead of drugs for many afflictions. They want safe, natural alternatives that work, and are easy to use. That's why herbs are so threatening to the drug people.

Relaxants like Valerian, sleep herbs like Hops and Passion Flower, and calming herbs such as Chamomile help you sleep, but the health store clerk can't tell you that. You can't be told which herbs are for sleep. You might not take your Halcion.

Murder yourself

The FDA has failed to protect us from Prozac, too. Prozac is the anti-depression drug with mental and physical side effects including, ironically, suicidal tendencies. Prozac will end your depression, one way or another.

Prozac is implicated in hundreds of violent outbursts,

including a 20 victim massacre in Kentucky. In TIME Magazine, the FDA said banning Prozac would financially harm the Eli Lilly Company. I wonder how many of us Prozac will harm.

In 1990, drug companies spent $10 billion on marketing — a billion dollars more than they spent on research. Drug prices are high because of sales and advertising expense, and exhorbitant profits — not because of research costs. They spend $5,000 per doctor, per year on promotion, while extorting money from the sick to pay for "research."

The "wonder drugs" you are waiting for may be farther off than we hoped, as more and more money is poured into marketing and the FDA trashes promising natural medicines.

Much drug research is to develop synthetic chemicals that resemble substances in herbs. The synthetic seldom works as well as the herb, but it can be patented. It takes forever for the chemists to catch up with Nature. Natural penicillin from the herb Hyssop was used for thousands of years before it was synthesized in a laboratory. Sick people shouldn't have to die waiting for the drug companies to get patents. They should have immediate access to the natural medicines and information they need to live.

The profits from outrageous drug prices support drug company stock in the face of falling sales, as Americans turn away from drugs and toward exercise and nutrition. "Baby boomers" are saying NO! to prescription drugs. The drug companies and the FDA want to outlaw natural medicines to eliminate competition. Natural products are hurting drug sales.

Today's 40-year-olds don't want to be junkies. They see a doctor for diagnosis, then buy natural medicines instead of drugs. The idea is to stay healthy with foods and medicines that are good for you. They "listen to their bodies" and don't hear them asking for drugs. Millions of drug prescriptions are written, but never filled.

More and more patients don't trust prescription drugs or their doctor's knowledge of them. When they read about side effects, they find things the doctor didn't tell them, didn't want them to know—perhaps didn't know himself. Who can you trust?...Yourself.

The government used to urge us to say NO! to drugs. They didn't mean legal drugs, but we took it that way. Now the FDA wants us to say YES!, but we know too much.

The American medical industry is run by allopathic doctors who believe illness is caused by germs that must be killed. They practice violent medicine using life-threatening drugs, radiation and surgery to kill the cause of illness. Allopathic treatment works well for some afflictions, badly for others. It is practiced all over the world, but most medical systems also use nutrition and other safe, gentle therapies to heal the body.

American M.D.s learn little about prevention or nutrition in medical school. Many think natural healing is an out-dated Third World concept not worthy of respect, even laughable. They seem to think natural health is a fad, only for the "health freaks." They are wrong.

There is a gigantic popular movement toward natural health maintenance and away from conventional medicine. Trust and confidence fall to new lows with each story about killer drugs, unnecessary surgery, failed medical devices and FDA indifference. We need protection from people who don't think ethics and our lives are as important as money and power.

Many doctors are threatened by herbs and other natural medicines they don't understand, so they treat them contemptuously. Herbs are "quaint" and old-fashioned. They may not hurt, but they certainly won't help because they aren't modern and "scientific."

The message is that drugs are better, even if they kill you, because they are scientific. This is a war against your illness and war is violent, so you can expect pain and side effects.

Wimps heal; real men kill. American medicine thinks they have to destroy the body to save it. That's why their treatments cause so many iatrogenic illnesses and can be financially ruinous and physically devastating.

Your only defense is to use food medicines and other

practices to stay healthy. Otherwise, you're dead meat.

The FDA says herbs cannot be accepted as medicines because they aren't scientific, but that's not the real reason. Herbs can't be patented, so the drug companies the FDA works for can't monopolize them. It has nothing to do with safety or efficacy or your health. It's money.

In 1991 the FDA declared an herbal extract from the California Yew Tree to be a drug and called it Taxol. This happened after the National Cancer Institute and Bristol-Myers Drug Company got a monopoly on the trees and the processing. Taxol is effective against cancer. There's money in it, so an herb becomes a drug and thousands of victims of breast, ovarian and lung cancer may be saved. If the trees couldn't be monopolized, these people could be denied the information about the herb by the FDA and permitted to die.

That's exactly what will happen to heart disease victims when the wonder herbs Cayenne, Garlic and Hawthorn are outlawed.

In the meantime, Bristol-Myers Squibb, the second largest drug company, is in charge of harvesting a precious medical resource. It takes 100 years for a California yew to reach 25 feet in height and one foot in diameter, its full size. There are millions of cancer patients and each patient needs the bark from six to eight trees. With only twenty million trees, there obviously won't be enough Taxol for every cancer patient who needs it. Yet experts estimate up to 75% of these trees are being wasted by carelessness and incompetence in processing and forest management and the FDA does nothing.

Maybe you can prevent your heart attack

The key to heart attack prevention is healthy, clean arteries and other circulatory channels. There are several ways to clean your plumbing.

Arteries have three layers: an inner and outer sheath with a muscle between. The muscle opens and closes the arteries. When you're stressed frightened, tired or on caffeine and other stimulating drugs, your arteries narrow and your blood pressure goes up. You get a shot of energy. If there is an obstruction in a coronary artery, a blood clot can shut off the flow, causing a heart attack.

Your heart is a hydraulic pump. When the flow of blood is shut off, it sucks air and convulses, tearing itself apart. My heart attack affected the power source, so it was like shutting the motor off. The pump just stopped. I stopped, too, but it started again and so did I. I was lucky that time.

Statistical studies show you are most likely to have a heart attack on Monday morning. It's a good time to load up on Cayenne. It keeps my arteries open and prevents blood clots that cause heart attacks. Garlic and Ginger also prevent blood clots by lowering the level of fibrin, the clotting material.

Hardening of the arteries is caused by deposits that build up on the inside wall of the artery and prevent it from opening and closing. Over time, these deposits harden like mud on a river bank. Recent medical studies show garlic oil penetrates hardened deposits, softening them so they can be washed away by the soapy vitamin A in Cayenne. That's why Cayenne and Garlic work well together cleaning your plumbing, lowering blood pressure and preventing heart attack.

Your blood flow is like a river. Irritants in your blood called free radicals attack an artery near your heart, causing a wound. The wound scabs over with minerals and becomes a snag that catches passing debris that builds up to block the artery.

You don't know it's happening because you can't feel it. You find out when you get angina or have your heart attack, like I did. This process begins at birth and goes on every day forever. Arterial deposits have been found in infants as young as 18 months. Serious arterial blockage was found in autopsies conducted on 18-year-old soldiers during the Korean War.

These deposits accumulate during your lifetime. Eventually you drop dead. The only solution is to clean them out every day. Dissolve the block. Heal the wound. Flush out the minerals to get rid of the snag.

Don't stop. Keep on cleaning every day, continuously

washing away the cholesterol, dissolving the hardened deposits, restoring circulation everywhere. Don't let the deposits get started. You can do it by taking Cayenne and Garlic every day. It's like eating soap. Garlic softens the hard deposits and gets rid of the cholesterol, while Cayenne makes the platelets slippery, so they wash away, and heals the sores on your artery walls. They work best when taken together.

Whatever works

There are other ways to keep your circulatory system clean. The process is called chelation, from a Greek word meaning "to grab." A chelate is something that attaches itself to foreign matter, so it can be washed away. When you wash your hands, the soap chelates or grabs the dirt and they go down the drain together.

Cayenne, Garlic and other herbs clean your arteries by chelation, as do vitamins A, C, and E, according to reseach conducted for the Heart Association. Certain kinds of fish oil chelate, too.

The Chinese tell us to eat 6 pecans or 3 onions every day to clean our arteries; the Iranians say 2 or more cloves of garlic with a parsley chaser. The French suggest 3 glasses of red wine daily with plenty of cheese and fattened goose liver. It seems to work for them.

Some holistic M.D.s in Minnesota have shown the arteries can be cleaned with peroxide. A small town doctor in Vermont wrote a book espousing vinegar and honey as a cleaning agent.

Intravenous Chelation Therapy is a cleansing procedure developed in 1893 that uses ethylene-diamine-tetra-acetic acid (EDTA), a synthetic amino acid. The EDTA is fed into the circulatory system intravenously to improve metabolic and circulatory function by removing toxic metals and other metallic ions. The procedure can take up to 20 treatments to complete, but it costs a fraction of surgery and entails very little risk. Also, chelation cleans the entire circulatory system, not just a few inches of coronary artery.

Another safe way to clean the arteries is with Lecithin. Experts say the choline in Lecithin liquifies cholesterol and dissolves deposits. Nutritionists recommend taking three rounded tablespoons of lecithin granules at one time every day for 12 days, with light exercise about two hours after you take it. It's called the 12-Day Flush. They recommend a tablespoon or two a day as a maintenance dose.

Lecithin is actually a type of water-soluable fat derived from eggs and soybeans, used in chocolate bars and many other food products. It makes water and oil mix.

The mechanical approach

There are many ways to clean your arteries and other circulatory channels — all superior to surgery. Surgical procedures like bypass and angioplasty are extremely dangerous, expensive and debilitating, often causing brain damage or other dreadful affliction. Surgery will never make you "as good as new" or even as good as you were before the operation.

Balloon angioplasty is another high-risk, low-benefit procedure sold as being safer and cheaper than bypass surgery. In it, a tube or catheter with a balloon on the end is snaked through an artery to a narrowed area near the heart. When in position, the balloon is inflated, pressing the block against the artery wall, opening the passage wider so more blood can get to the heart.

Balloon angioplasty works on the same principal as the equally unscientific "fat bandage" advertised in movie magazines when I was a kid. The "fat bandage" was a long cloth boa. Wrap it tightly around yourself, hold your breath, then unwrap it and be thin for two or three minutes.

With balloon angioplasty, the inflated balloon inside the artery presses the obstruction against the artery wall to open the blood channel wider. It stays open for a while, just like the fat bandage makes you thin for a while.

Balloon angioplasty stretches and damages the artery muscle so severely it collapses about one-third of the time—

then you need an emergency bypass or you die.

Hospitals keep a complete bypass surgical team on hand during the angioplasty because of the likelihood of arterial collapse. If you get off the angioplasty table alive, you remain at risk of sudden collapse and death for at least a year afterward. It costs about $12,000, if you don't need an emergency bypass or suffer some other complication. It is a high-risk temporary fix at best.

If you liked the "fat bandage," you'll love the stent, the mesh and the coil. These tiny contraptions are inserted into an artery to hold it open. They quickly become artery-damaging obstructions themselves, catching cholesterol and other material to form new blockages. They become so imbedded in the artery they cannot be removed and constitute a new problem much more serious than the condition they are supposed to correct.

Then there's the laser angioplasty. The laser beam zaps the obstruction and melts part of it away. The problem is that when your heart beats, your artery moves, so it's easy to zap the artery itself and melt a hole in it. Goodbye. Laser angioplasty is only safe if you are already dead.

The "roto-rooter" is another example of medical mechanical genius at work. I think it was conceived by a plumber from the New York City Sewer Department. Once again, they snake a catheter through your artery to an obstructed area near your heart. Then they turn on the power and little blades cut away the obstruction faster than your Salad Shooter can slice a tomato. Another triumph! One problem: the little chunks of debris can stick in inconvenient places like your brain. Also, the drilled-out opening begins closing again at once. And what if the cute little cutter takes a chunk out of your artery? Let's not talk about that.

The stress cardiogram is the first step on the treadmill to disaster for most cardiac patients. It is a diagnostic procedure that can kill you. I had one in May 1978 and didn't recover for six months. I think it caused my heart attack.

Usually you have a resting cardiogram first, which records your heart rhythm but often shows nothing unusual. So you put on tennis shoes and shorts and go back for your stress cardiogram.

In a stress cardiogram, you walk or run on a treadmill with sensors taped to your body, until you collapse or an "irregularity" is detected. Often, the "irregularity" is a heart attack.

During the cardiogram, your doctor sits by the treadmill and "monitors" your heart and lung functions, which is like starting a fire and then watching the building burn down. People die during stress cardiograms because inept doctors start heart attacks they can't stop. Worst of all, much of the data provided by the cardiogram is wrong or misinterpreted.

The stress cardiogram I had was a mistake that nearly killed me. It's a deadly diagnostic procedure that doesn't work. Never again.

The porch roof Dick Quinn cleared after his first dose of Cayenne pepper.

"American medicine grows because its major functions are economic and political, rather than therapeutic."

John L. McKnight
<u>Comparative Medicine</u>

5

KNOWLEDGE
IS THE KEY

E ven a diagnostic angiogram has a risk that far outweighs benefit in my opinion. The idea is to look at the inside of your heart and arteries with a tiny TV camera and measure blood flow, pressure and other factors. They run a fine tube or catheter through an artery and into your heart. It is a sales procedure used to market angioplasty and bypass by showing the customer narrowed and obstructed arteries.

It's also a power trip for the cardiologist who loves the life-and-death thrill of being in your heart. But it is an invasive diagnostic procedure with significant risk. You can die during an angiogram. The catheter can tear or bruise the artery, causing massive problems including death. You may be seriously allergic to the dye they squirt into your heart to track blood flow. The procedure could cause a heart attack or seizure. Angiograms are risky and the resulting diagnosis may be wrong because the extent of arterial blockage cannot be precisely measured.

When the cardiologist told me my artery was 98% blocked, it was just a very unscientific estimate, perhaps influenced by the desire to sell me a bypass.

Sales techniques for marketing coronary surgery are taught at some hospitals. Sales reps learn to lie about the "benefits" of surgery and use fear, guilt and hope to sell.

With male patients, the surgery salesperson suggests to the wife that she will be a widow and the family fatherless unless he has surgery. It will make him "as good as new" and prevent a heart attack. Those are key lies.

The pain and risk, the mental and physical cost are passed over. It's "a simple procedure." They do it all the time: No problem.

The patient is presented as a stubborn, but lovable oaf who doesn't know what's good for him and is too macho to care. It's his wife's job to sell him — which she does.

They are a family of victims who face bitter, bitter disappointment and financial ruin, but really want to believe this will work. They're afraid to ask what might go wrong.

A few years ago, I met a woman at a party whose father was about to have a triple bypass. He didn't want it, but she had been sold. This would relieve her of guilt.

She had accepted the risk to him and his death. He hadn't. She saw bypass surgery as a neat, clean, accepted way to resolve her guilt and anxiety by putting the Angel of Death in charge.

Cut him open and let it happen according to the will of God. Whatever will be, will be. Goodbye, Dad. It's time you dodder off.

I strongly suggested that her father's wishes be honored, as he would suffer the pain and do the dying. Seek a second opinion. Make sure this is not a mistake, for his sake. Just present the facts and do as he wishes.

If bypass surgery is as sure and easy as she and the cardiologist say, they should each have it first to show their faith in Modern Medical Science and reassure her father.

She became angry when I suggested her father might have a stroke or other serious complications from the operation and she wouldn't want to be responsible. She assailed me for lacking faith in our sainted medical doctors, then ended the conversation.

When last I heard, her father had survived the bypass and the resulting stroke. By now he probably has use of his left arm and leg. Therapy is helping him speak again.

There is a very high risk of brain damage from the heart-lung machine during bypass surgery. In 1978, doctors usually bypassed two or three arteries; now four and five artery bypasses are common, so the operation takes longer. That means more time for the heart-lung machine to put bubbles, plastic particles and other debris into your blood to cause brain damage. More time for the machine's rough plastic hoses to bruise the blood cells, so they clump together and cause a stroke.

Like selling used cars, but not as ethical

There is another risk to you that is implicit in all coronary surgery. Payola. Many doctors get kick-backs from the cardiologist, the hospital, the surgeons and, possibly, other people. You are the product being sold. It is accepted procedure to pay commissions. Surely your doctor will take his cut. Does he need money for something, a car or trip perhaps? Does he see you as a person or a profit source?

Would your doctor sell you surgery you don't need for a commission he does need?

The coronary industry has spent a fortune promoting business for its drugs and surgery. The Stanford University Medical Center proposed a "retreat" for referring doctors at its swank Pebble Beach resort on the Pacific coast. Tickets to big league games and other events, lavishly catered dinners, free rent, cash payments disguised as speaking honorariums, trips — kick-backs come in many forms from hospitals, specialists and medical suppliers.

Drug companies also pay prescribing doctors kick-backs. Doctors who push the right drugs get expensive dinners, paid speaking engagements, trips to the South Seas, gifts - even cash. Drug companies start selling in medical school.

Apparently, the pay-offs are O.K. with the FDA and AMA. Who needs ethics, principles or honor when you have money?

All the big-money coronary procedures pose serious threats to your arterial system. You need your arteries — all of them. You came without replacement parts, so you have to get through life with what you have.

The rich are at risk

If you are wealthy or have very good health insurance coverage, you are at greatest risk.

You want "the best money can buy," so you will buy every miserable surgery on the list. You'll be cut, drugged and bled to death, literally.

You want the best, but it's hard to be sure you're getting it, so you will settle for the most. Expect the full treatment.

Surgeons vary widely in competence. The best kill 1.9% of their patients during bypass, the worst kill 9.9%; some hospitals lose 11.9%. There is no way to tell the best from the worst, no matter how much money you have. Good luck.

There are about 360,000 coronary bypass operations in the U.S. every year. The average cost: $40,000. Gross annual sales: $14,400,000,000. I said Fourteen Billion Four Hundred Million.

If you are a piece of meat with money, you can expect several coronary bypass operations, each more devastating than the last. You'll play chemical roulette, not knowing the more drugs you take, the shorter your life. In the end, treatment will kill you.

The secret: keep your plumbing clean

You and I have thousands of miles of arteries, veins, capillaries and arterials—all of which must be kept clean. As I learned from my 1978 heart attack, you need every inch. Surgery only deals with a tiny part of the system and it doesn't even fix that. So surgery fails.

Coronary bypass, angioplasty and gimmicks like the laser, stent and the "roto rooter" do not extend your life, improve your quality of life or prevent a heart attack. Statistics prove they do not benefit the patient, so they don't work. There is nothing in them for you but pain, depression, ruin and death.

I keep my arteries clean with herbs. They're cheap, easy to use and they work.

It's easy. I just get up every morning and put some capsules in my mouth on the way to the bathroom. If it were any more complicated or took more time, I wouldn't do it. The capsules I can do easily, so I have taken them every day since 1978. I'll stop when I decide it's time to silt-up and die. That may be a while.

When I swallow the capsules every morning, I know it's done. The good guys are in there now, cleaning and scouring, working for me every minute. That's nice to know.

I consider Dr. John Christopher the patron saint of Cayenne, the herb that's most important to my health. Had Christopher not lived, I would not be alive today, because I would never have heard of Cayenne or what it can do. He told the lady by the lake and she told me.

I have learned a lot about Cayenne from my years of study, but it began with Christopher and his books.

Cayenne isn't really a pepper or even a vegetable. It's a fruit and a Capsicum. The botanical description of a Capsicum is "bag of seeds." Tomatoes are also Capsicums.

Cayenne was used medicinally in ancient Egypt 5,000 years ago and is found in some of the oldest tomb art. It didn't get to Europe until 1493, when Columbus returned from his first voyage to the New World. He discovered it along the Cayenne River on the largest of the Cayenne Islands off the North coast of South America. The island was later to be home for the French penal colony called Devil's Island.

Cayenne was found to have remarkable healing and disinfecting powers by the ship's doctor while still on the voyage. Crewmen on wooden ships get many slivers, which often become infected. Cayenne killed infections and stopped even the most profuse bleeding instantly. It was also effective against scurvy, because of its vitamin C.

Modern researchers have confirmed many of Cayenne's medicinal powers. Dermatologists at the University of California, Davis, have discovered it causes surgical wounds to heal faster than antibiotics. Researchers at West Virginia University and the Loma Linda School of Medicine in California have found Cayenne fights cancer, too. It prevents the liver from turning the polyaromatic hydrocarbons in smoked and broiled meat and the aflatoxins in peanut butter into carcinogens.

Cayenne makes weight control easier by causing the body to burn up to 25 percent more calories every day, according to scientists in Great Britain and Japan.

When we eat Cayenne, nerve endings secrete Substance P, which alerts the brain to pain. In response to the Substance P pain signal, other nerve cells secrete endorphines, the body's pain killers, which act like morphine to stop the pain and convey a sense of well-being. Cayenne and Capsaicin, its primary active ingredient, are used to kill pain from shingles and many other chronic ailments and have also been found effective against psoriasis.

After hearing that Cayenne causes pain and then kills it, I decided to experiment. I put about one half teaspoon of very hot Cayenne in a small glass of beer and stirred vigorously. The first drink was the hottest thing I ever put in my mouth. Molten lead couldn't feel hotter. The alcohol in the beer had dissolved the hot, oily Capsaicin and stripped the protective mucous from my mouth, tongue and throat, exposing the tender tissue to incredible heat. It felt like my lips were on fire. I could imagine my teeth melting.

Water made it worse. So did plain beer. Finally I just decided to drink the rest of my flaming concoction, no matter what. I'd sacrifice my mouth to science.

My second swallow didn't seem quite so hot. I drank a little more. There was even less pain. By the time I finished half the glass, the burning stopped completely and I felt pretty good, though I noticed some light perspiration.

I had passed through the "wall of fire" and proven to myself that Cayenne not only causes pain, it kills pain.

You can make a super-hot beverage with juice, too. Just put Cayenne in juice, stir and let stand. The longer it stands, the hotter it gets, as it draws the Capsaicin from the Cayenne. Put the mixture in the refrigerator for a few hours and you'll see what hot is all about.

Many ways have been suggested to stop your mouth from burning when you eat hot food. Some recommend orange juice or mango juice, both popular in India. Others say the butterfat in milk or ice cream mixes with the oily Capsaicin and carries it away. One person I know eats ice. But I think the solution is to eat more Cayenne and trigger its painkilling action. It's a daunting thing to consider when you are already on fire, but it works.

Cayenne is powerful and can be painful, but it doesn't damage tissue, so it makes an ideal spray for personal protection from violent people and animals. Cayenne spray stops the most determined assailant on contact, causing temporary blindness, collapse and loss of consciousness with no permanent damage.

I got some Cayenne in my eye one afternoon. My eye watered so profusely, it soaked two handkerchiefs, my shirt and a towel. The watering went on for hours, but did no damage. My eye wasn't even bloodshot when it finally stopped, but I had new respect for Cayenne.

When Columbus discovered Cayenne he called it Red Pepper, because he had been looking for Black Pepper. He brought Cayenne to Europe in 1493 and it quickly spread East, across the continent, to Hungary, where the heat was bred out and it became Paprika. Paprika is often mixed with Cayenne to make a milder blend for cooking and to use in some health products.

Today, Cayenne isn't even grown on the Cayenne Islands or anywhere in the Caribbean, but is found in Louisiana and the American Southwest, Asia, Africa and one area of Mexico.

Dr. John Christopher tells of a village in Mexico where great quantities of Cayenne are eaten and used in a local beverage. Villagers are known for their long, healthy lives.

Once, years ago, a party of hunters from the village left on a long trip through the mountains. Along the way, a member of the party was bitten by a snake and died. It was such a rocky area, the body couldn't be buried, so it was left beside the trail to be picked up the next day.

When the hunters returned, they found the body undisturbed, but surrounded by hungry vultures. The man had eaten so much Cayenne, the vultures wouldn't touch him.

Researchers at the University of Pennsylvania discovered a pigeon in India that eats Cayenne as protection from predators. The pigeon literally becomes too hot to eat.

Cayenne is safe, but you better respect it. It can cause an upset stomach. To settle your stomach, eat bread, crackers or rolls with water, milk or other cold drink.

When Cayenne is drunk in juice or eaten on food, it rarely causes discomfort.

Since Cayenne detoxifies the liver and other organs, it can cause the "burning dumps" for up to 3 days, though some people don't have them at all. Your kidneys, liver and other organs may contain very powerful, caustic poisons they have filtered out of your blood. Now you can get rid of them.

According to Dr. Christopher, African Birdseye Cayenne is the most effective medicinally. These are tiny peppers from Sierra Leon in West Africa that are actually planted by birds. The birds eat the peppers and plant the seeds for next year's crop in their droppings. The peppers grow wild, without cultivation of any kind. They're tolerated like a weed, not cultivated. At harvest time, they are gathered up and sold.

If you have a heart condition like I do, you have a big, bad enemy, so you need a big, bad friend. Cayenne is just the friend I need.

I have studied herbs since 1978 and found there are many that can help me. They seem to work best when combined. Cayenne works better when combined with Ginger, its facilitator. Onion facilitates Garlic, helping it work better. Myrrh facilitates the anti-biotic herb Goldenseal. And everything seems to work better if you power it with Cayenne, the universal companion herb.

These herbs synergize when blended, so each herb becomes up to 10 times more powerful. Synergistic herbs work together with actions that complement one another, making each stronger and more effective.

Cayenne and Garlic synergize to regulate my blood pressure and clean out my arteries. Cayenne and Hawthorn synergize to strengthen my heart and give me more stamina. Valerian synergizes with Passion Flower and Cayenne to regulate my heartbeat, so it doesn't bang around when I've had a long day.

One day several years ago, my wife Paula collapsed while biking. She was weak, dizzy, light-headed and faint. It took an hour for her to recover enough to walk the short way home.

We later learned she had an attack of atrial fibrillation, involving an irregular heartbeat and blood flow. She began taking Valerian and Cayenne, the herbs used to prevent fibrillation, and the attacks stopped.

Herbs regulate blood pressure

Many herbs regulate blood pressure, but Garlic and Cayenne are most widely prescribed for blood pressure control. Celery Seed, Valerian, Passion Flower, Marijuana (called Hemp by many herbalists), Gotu Kola and Skullcap are said to lower high blood pressure, while Parsley, Dandelion and Brigham Tea raise low blood pressure.

Most of these herbs work by cleansing the arteries. Marijuana relaxes the artery to lower blood pressure, just as it lowers fluid pressure in the eye to prevent blindness from glaucoma.

Valerian is a wonderful herb for the heart. It relaxes me and eases stress better than Valium without danger of overdose or addiction. Originally from Eastern Europe, Valerian has been used safely for several thousand years. It is recognized as an effective heart herb in every European country.

Valerian is a root that smells like dirty socks. In 17th century Europe, bathing was considered immodest, so Valerian oil became popular as a perfume. It was the only thing that smelled worse than the people. Cats and rats both love Valerian. In fact, the Pied Piper is said to have used it to draw the rats away from the village of Hamline.

Valerian's odor comes from the acids that make it work. The stronger it is, the worse it smells.

The name for Valium, the addictive drug, was said to have been inspired by Valerian, but the two have absolutely no connection. Valerian is much more effective as a relaxant and is not dangerous in large doses or addictive like Valium. If a drug company could patent it, Valerian would be available everywhere.

Hawthorn is another remarkable heart herb from Europe. The German FDA has registered over 40 heart medicines made with it. Typically, a heart attack results in damage to the heart muscle. Capillaries are broken in the attack, so a part of the heart muscle is deprived of blood and atrophies or dies. European studies show Hawthorn re-opens damaged capillaries to restore circulation and resuscitate damaged muscle, so the heart recovers.

Hawthorn is used by European doctors to treat and prevent angina pectoris, lower cholesterol and blood pressure, correct cardiac insufficiency and restore lost heart function. Though not yet even recognized as safe by the FDA, Hawthorn is a widely prescribed heart medicine in Europe. The berries are used to make the most popular jelly there.

The poisonous herb Fox Glove is the source of Digitalis, the heart stimulant. Few herbalists use Fox Glove because it's so dangerous. They know Lily of the Valley stimulates more safely and helps the heart repair defective valves. Recent studies show Digitalis causes a dramatic increase in death from sudden heart failure.

People often "underdose" when taking medicinal herbs because they don't realize herbs are foods, not drugs. They are highly nutritious, many are very powerful, and most are safe. Onion, Parsley and many others have no point at which they become poisonous. If you eat too many aspirins, you will die; if you eat too much Cayenne, you will get a stomach ache. Herbs can be powerful without being poisonous.

Herbs promote health with natural vitamins, minerals and other nutrients you need every day. Health maintenance with herbs is a long-term proposition. You feed your body little doses of natural, user-friendly nutrients every day, so it gets a continuous supply of the things it needs to work well and be happy. You take your herbs every day until you decide to die.

There are many systems of medicine in the world and nearly all of them use herbs. Cayenne and other Western herbs are vegetables, but Chinese herbalists also use animal parts such as deer antler and water snake oil. Conventional medicine as practiced in America has had many successes, and many failures. Its successes come from dedication, intelligence and concern; its failures from arrogance, greed and indifference.

American treatment for heart disease seriously harms the patient and does not extend life. After millions spent on cancer, U.S. medicine seems even farther from success. Not a single AIDS patient has ever been cured and there has been no success with Alzheimer's disease. Maybe it's time to try some natural medicines.

Ironically, cancer, AIDS and heart disease are three afflictions reserved by the FDA for conventional treatments that often don't work. They are high-buck diseases American medicine makes a killing on, medically and financially.

There are safe, natural treatments for these diseases that hold great promise, like California Yew and Chaparral for cancer, Cayenne and Garlic for the arteries, Hawthorn for the heart, Gotu Kola for Alzheimer's. These herbs are easy to use, cheap, effective and safe. They are the ideal alternative to drugs. But maybe they're just too good to be legal.

There are thousands of herbs, but only a few "super herbs" such as Garlic, Cayenne and Valerian. They are used in many formulas because they are so broadly beneficial. Other herbs have one overwhelming area of benefit, such as Hawthorn for the heart.

Vitamins, minerals and other ingredients in herbs work together to get the job done. For example, Cayenne aids circulation by opening the arteries and cleansing the circulatory system. To do this, it has five different types of capsaicin and lots of soapy beta carotene (Vitamin A) to scour and wash away plaque and cholesterol, heal lesions and restore arterial flexibility. Valerian is ideally suited to deal with stress, depression and insomnia. It is one of the richest herbs in natural calcium, the mineral despondent people most need.

In the 1980s, herbal extracts and concentrates became popular as "soft drugs." The concentrator washes the oils out of the herbs with a solvent like ether or alcohol, then mixes the oils with some of the herb to get a concentrate. Oil from 12 pounds of herbs mixed with 1 pound of the whole herb makes a 12 to 1 concentrate.

The theory is that the "active" ingredients are oil based, so extracting and concentrating these oils in a formulation, makes it more powerful. The problem: some of the nutrients that are discarded are needed to make the extract safe and effective, so the extract or concentrate doesn't have the same benefits as the herb.

For example, Cayenne lowers blood pressure, but extracted Capsaicin raises it. Studies have shown Valerian concentrate to be unsafe, but Valerian herb is absolutely safe. Many desirable vitamins, minerals and other nutrients are destroyed by the heat and solvent or thrown away with the waste.

Poppies are safe, opium is not; coca leaves are safe, cocaine is not. All are concentrates.

Herbs already are concentrated. You cannot improve on an herb. Concentraters make the same mistake drug companies make and sometimes poison the patient.

Your body doesn't use synthetic vitamins efficiently because it can't recognize them. But the vitamins and minerals in herbs are "naturally occurring," so your body can recognize and use them all. Synthetic vitamins and minerals can be toxic. For example, a leading cause of calls to the Poison Control Center in Minneapolis is poisoning from synthetic vitamin A in children's vitamins. Kids want to be big and strong, as advertised, so they overdose.

Synthetic vitamins and minerals are chemically identical to natural vitamins and minerals but differ in molecular structure, so your body may not know what they are. As little as 5% of a synthetic may actually be used by your body. Much of the rest is eliminated safely but some is stored in your arteries, brain and other vital organs where it can cause problems.

Drugs are often synthetic copies of substances in herbs. Many of the cold medicines sold in drug stores contain synthetic replications of active ingredients found in Cayenne.

Over 25% of prescription drugs are also from herbs. But thousands of valuable herbal medicines can't be synthesized. The healing agents they contain are only found in the whole herb.

Many nutritional ingredients in herbs have not yet been identified by the drug chemists. They can't be synthesized.

We all self-medicate. Nearly everybody takes vitamins, uses food as medicine or exercises. Herbs are super foods. We all should know more about them and use them more often, but the FDA and A.M.A. keep getting in the way.

The number one cause of death in America is legal drugs. Drugs can't keep us healthy because they are all poisons. The "side effect" is the hangover you get from being poisoned. Since drugs are poisons, they don't heal like herbs and other natural medicines.

Radiation is another type of medical poison. It has always been known that radiation causes cancer, yet X-rays have been over-used for years in hospitals, medical clinics and dental offices. Mammography has been promoted as a profitable business, over safer methods of breast cancer detection. Early detection is vital since the disease is fatal unless caught early, so the number of mammography X-ray units has grown dramatically. Meanwhile, the incidence of breast cancer has grown, too. Ironically, studies show the highly profitable X-ray mammography used to detect breast cancer may actually cause it. American medicine has an ethical dilemma as we realize breast cancer is an Iatrogenic disease.

Iatrogenic (doctor caused) illnesses have grown to become a whole new category of disease. Many patients in U.S. hospitals suffer from Iatrogenic illness caused by drugs, surgery or radiation used to treat or diagnose the original illness.

If my doctor didn't know about natural medicines, I'd fire him.

Maybe you should tell your doctor to learn more about safe alternatives to drugs and surgery, find a doctor who already knows, or become your own doctor as I did. To help yourself feel good and stay well, herbs and other safe, natural foods should be part of your health arsenal. You deserve every chance to live a longer, happier, healthier life.

There are herbs for every illness, no matter how serious. I use only herbs to treat my heart condition and haven't had a drug prescription for anything since shortly after my 1978 heart attack. Herbs can prevent cancer and heart attack, kill tumors, lower cholesterol and blood pressure, grow hair, treat AIDS, arthritis, asthma, angina and every other ailment. There are herbs for every organ and every physical and mental affliction known. There may well be herbs that will help you and those you love, if you can find out about them. I'll tell you as much as I can.

6

1988: MY TENTH ANNIVERSARY

After my 1978 recovery, I continued to work as a freelance writer of ads, letters, magazine stories — anything that would earn a buck. I read every book I could find on herbs and natural healing. It was amazing how many medicines I found that I had never heard of before — all purported to have unique healing powers. I told my friends about them, but very few took me seriously.

In 1988, I realized Cayenne had kept me alive for 10 years. This was definitely not just the "placebo effect" — the stuff really worked. I was determined to tell the world, whether it wanted to listen or not. I naively thought the medical people would want to know, too.

I couldn't buy manufactured products with the kind of Cayenne and other herbs I used, so I decided to make them myself.

I would have to learn how to be a manufacturer. I was 52 years old and had been a writer for 30 years. It was time to do something new.

When I began taking Cayenne, I just bought the low powered culinary variety in a grocery store. It had only a few thousand heat units of potency, but it worked fine for me at first. I soon came to feel that stronger was better. I tried 40,000 heat unit Cayenne from health stores and then discovered some even stronger 80,000 heat unit Cayenne at the local food cooperative.

I began taking Garlic and Lecithin in addition to Cayenne. There was no identifiable health benefit from the Garlic, but the Lecithin seemed to boost my stamina. Lecithin granules are more potent than capsules, so I took those. I was still searching for a way to "tell the world" about my experience. I decided to write a book about the herbs I had found. The book and herbs could be sold by mail order. I ran a mail order ad in the June 1988 issue of *Grit* Magazine selling Cayenne, Lecithin and the book I intended to write. The ad didn't produce a single order, but an elderly lady from Kansas sent me one dollar and asked for information. I sent her dollar back with a letter about the benefits of Cayenne and Lecithin.

About this time, I read an article on AIDS. Some of the AIDS symptoms reminded me of my own when I was dying after my bypass, so I thought Cayenne might help them, too. I had just found some even stronger Cayenne in a wholesale catalog that had 90,000 heat units of potency.

I took some capsules of my extra-strong Cayenne to an AIDS support group and buying club in Minneapolis. My Cayenne was much more powerful than any they had taken before. They each took nine capsules of Cayenne a day and reported a dramatic increase in energy, fewer colds and flu symptoms. One user told me the Cayenne gave him enough energy to go back to work. Several of them said it sometimes caused burning in the stomach and lower intestinal tract, but the energy was worth it.

In what could be the most important discovery of all, several members of the group theorized that Cayenne might prevent the HIV virus from becoming AIDS. It seemed to have that effect but no one could be sure. The virus can become AIDS in a few months, but sometimes it takes years. If we could find out what delays it, maybe we could put it off forever.

The HIV-infected people in their group who had gone longest without infection met one evening to look for a common trait that might explain it. Several had the HIV virus for more than eight years. They could find only one thing: they all ate very hot Asian food several times a week. Maybe the Cayenne they ate delayed AIDS symptoms. No research is being done on Cayenne because there is so little interest in unpatentable natural medicines among people with research funds. Cayenne can't be patented or monopolized.

The 90,000 heat unit Cayenne didn't bother me, but it was too hot for most people who tried it, including my friend Al Watson.

On the first day, Al had the dreaded "burning dumps," as the Cayenne de-toxified his system and dumped the poisons. The Cayenne also sometimes gave him a stomach ache or heartburn, but he enjoyed the energy lift so much he kept taking it.

In August 1988, Al took my Cayenne capsules to the Sebeka Town Festival. He returned to tell me I was now the most cursed person in Northern Minnesota.

Something had to be done to make high-powered Cayenne user-friendly. I had to find a way to take out the pain, but keep the power.

I kept looking for stronger and stronger Cayenne. It was keeping me alive, and I wanted all the energy I could get. I found a source of the African Birdseye Peppers, recommended by Dr. John Christopher. I ground them up with my kitchen blender and began taking several big capsules of them every day. At first, I didn't have any problem, though they were rated at nearly 150,000 heat units.

One morning I took three or four capsules of the African Cayenne while I was hurriedly dressing for a business meeting. There was no time to eat breakfast. I put on a suit and tie and rushed outside.

I had just sat down in the car when I began to feel a little queasy. I was about to have the Mother of all pepper attacks.

The nausea intensified. I began to feel warm. Then came stomach cramps which grew more and more painful. They seemed to last forever. Suddenly I burst into a sweat that was so intense, my shirt, suit and stockings were instantly drenched. Even my necktie was wet. The handkerchief in my back pocket was soaked. My socks seemed to slosh in my shoes when I walked back to my apartment. I took a shower, put on dry clothes, changed shoes and went to my meeting, a wiser man.

This was the Cayenne I was looking for.

The African Cayenne seemed to work even better when I blended it with Cayenne from India. They went well together. Plants from different places have different nutritional characteristics, so I felt the blend gave me a better balance of vitamins and minerals without sacrificing power.

One day in the Fall of 1988, I discovered almost by accident that Ginger and Lecithin make Cayenne easier on the body. Ginger stimulates the stomach so it can handle the heat. Lecithin makes the hot Capsaicin blend with water and other things in your stomach so it's gentler and faster acting. I was on my way.

1989: The Heart Foods Company begins

It took me a year to refine the formulas, name them and design labels. I had decided to call the company Heart Foods when I ran the *Grit* Magazine ad in 1988, now I looked for a heart to use as a logo. I first thought of a heart with a plant growing from it. A terrible idea.

The human heart isn't really heart shaped. It looks like something you'd find in the butcher shop next to pig snouts and sheep brains. One night I awoke with a mental picture of a green Valentine's heart. Perfect.

I spent hours in liquor stores, drug stores, supermarkets and health food stores looking at labels. I even went to California to look at products in retail stores there. Later I found a distributor in Minneapolis who said he might sell my line to health food stores, when I had a line to sell.

I decided to use a big heart on the label, so it could be seen on the store shelf. I wanted to use names and colors that suggested what each product was for.

I named my most powerful Cayenne formula Power Caps and gave it a red heart. I made Power Caps for myself. They keep me alive and give me the energy and enthusiasm I need to do things, like start the Heart Foods Company at age 52. Power Caps are my favorite, my mean old junkyard dog. They have more of my 100,000 heat unit blend of African and Indian Cayenne than our other Cap. They also have Hawthorn for my heart and Ginger to give me a lift and put the fire out.

Thinking Caps have a golden yellow heart. I made them for my grandfather, who had Alzheimer's Disease when he died 60 years ago. Too bad he didn't have Thinking Caps then. The Gotu Kola and Ginkgo Biloba they contain might have helped. The people of China and India have used those two herbs to prevent senility and slow aging for centuries. Gotu Kola is called "healing grass" in India. It's a mental stimulant that contains no caffeine.

In 60 years, no progress has been made on the treatment of Alzheimer's with drugs, but Ginkgo Biloba has shown promising results in some medical studies. Gotu Kola is rich in organic aluminum, which may remove inorganic aluminum from the brain to relieve the symptoms. Since Gotu Kola cannot be patented, no research is being conducted on it.

Happy Caps are for people who work too hard, like Paula. They have Valerian, Catnip and our powerful Cayenne for stress with a cheerful orange heart on the label.

The color purple is for sleep and so are Night Caps. They help you relax with Valerian, dull aches and pains with Skullcap, and induce sleep with Passion Flower.

In May 1989, I introduced Power Caps, Thinking Caps, Happy Caps and Night Caps to the Minneapolis distributor. He promptly got them into several health food stores, where they were slow but encouraging sellers. It's hard to sell something when you can't tell customers what it's used for.

Later that summer, I added Heart Food Caps to the Heart Foods line as our product for cardiovascular health. The formula combines my strong African/Indian Cayenne blend with Garlic and Hawthorn, the herb used in Germany to regenerate damaged heart tissue.

The herbs in Heart Food Caps clean arteries, lower cholesterol and blood pressure, dissolve blood clots, stop angina and safely stimulate the heart without speeding up the heartbeat. Cayenne Garlic and Hawthorn synergize with each other, so each has more healing power when combined.

Getting started as a manufacturer

When I began the Heart Foods Company, I looked for someone to fill the capsules for me. There are very few pharmaceutical companies in Minnesota. I found several custom manufacturers in other states, but they wouldn't work with the extra-hot Cayenne I used. I realized I would have to manufacture the products myself. I looked through manufacturers' directories at the library, but couldn't find capsule-filling machines, so I filled the capsules by hand.

My first factory was in the living room of my apartment. Al Watson and I filled capsules and bottled them. Paula helped grind herbs to make the formulas. The apartment smelled like an Italian restaurant because of all the herbs.

One day I was in the kitchen grinding African Birdseye Cayenne when a friend called. I got involved in the conversation and forgot the Cayenne until the grinder got very hot. When I took the top off the grinder, an ominous brown cloud rose slowly from it and stood there, like an evil creature.

Not thinking, I looked into the grinder and inadvertently inhaled. My knees buckled. I nearly passed out. For a few minutes, I couldn't breathe. My eyes burned and watered so much I couldn't see. I fumbled round until I found the switch to turn on the exhaust fan over the stove, crawled out of the kitchen and opened the balcony door and the windows to get rid of the fumes. Then I went into the bathroom and washed my face until I could open my eyes.

I kept looking for a machine to fill capsules, so I could set up a real factory. But capsule filling machines cost too much and herbs were too sticky to work in most of them. I didn't have any money, anyway.

I sold a few bottles of the Caps, but couldn't get big sales without money to advertise.

Financing the company with Tick Attack

It was June 1989 and the biggest scare of the summer was Lyme Disease carried by deer ticks. The Caps were in some stores but it seemed no one knew it. They were selling so slowly they might get kicked out. Customers didn't know much about Cayenne and couldn't be told what it did for health. I had no money to advertise. It looked grim for Heart Foods.

One night I was in a Mexican restaurant with my wife Paula and I mentioned that I knew how to make a pretty good tick repellent from herbs. I had found the recipe in an old book and used it on my St. Bernard, Keily, years before I ever thought of herbs as medicine. It was so safe a child could drink it. In fact, it tasted pretty good.

Paula urged me to make some at once, and sell it in cooperatives and health stores as a new, non-toxic repellent called Tick Attack.

I changed the recipe to make it smell and work better, designed and printed a label, brewed and bottled the first batch and delivered it to my distributor in 20 days. The Tick Attack fermented, so the bottles blew up, but I fixed that in the second batch.

It sold on sight in the health stores and cooperatives. Everybody wanted Tick Attack because it didn't have any toxic chemicals, had a wonderful aroma and wasn't sticky or greasy. People could use it safely on their pets, their kids and themselves.

The primary ingredients were Tick Weed and European Pennyroyal, both insect-repelling members of the mint family that are also used to treat indigestion. Lavender and Lemon Grass smelled great and boosted repelling power. I also used Quassia, an herbal wood from Surinam in South America that was discovered by a slave named Quassi. He won his freedom in 1750 by telling his master about its remarkable antiseptic properties, so they named the herb after him.

Quassia is a bitter herb used to aid digestion. George Washington kept his drinking water in a pail made of Quassia and drank it as a stomach tonic. It also kills flies.

Tick Attack seems to act as a deterrent, not a repellent. Apparently, it works with the skin chemistry to discourage ticks from biting. Tick Attack doesn't kill or repel, it just spoils the tick's appetite.

Tick Attack was an instant hit in the health stores and food cooperatives. Everyone wanted bug products that didn't kill their children or themselves.

I made the Tick Attack in plastic garbage cans in my bathtub at my apartment. I brewed about 40 gallons of Tick Attack "tea" in the evening, let it cool overnight, then put on a swimming suit and bottled it in the bathtub, washing off the bottles (and myself) under the shower. I dried the bottles, labeled them and delivered the finished Tick Attack while another batch was brewing.

My apartment got a little humid and the paint began peeling off the ceiling of the bathroom, but it was an otherwise smooth operation. Nothing is entirely problem-free.

My son Devin was in town, so I rented a second apartment and hired him to make it with me. The summer tick season would be over soon, so there was no time to set up a real factory. Our production was over 200 gallons a day.

People bought Tick Attack because it did not contain DEET, the poisonous chemical repellent that was developed during the Viet Nam War. DEET is absorbed through the skin and is said to have caused encephalitis, brain damage and death among children. It is especially dangerous to put clothes on after applying DEET, because the chemical toxins can't evaporate and more is absorbed by your body.

I used some of the money from Tick Attack sales to boost my production of the Caps by buying a manually operated machine to fill capsules. It could only fill 2,700 capsules an hour, but it was well worth the $4,200 it cost. Cap sales at health food stores were still slow and the tick season was winding down. I had to find a way to sell more Caps.

1990: We discover catalogs

The Heart Foods Company barely survived after the Tick Attack season ended in the Fall of 1989. Our Cap sales in November and December were about $150 per month. Power Caps and Thinking Caps were our best sellers in health food stores, but our overall sales were poor because we couldn't tell people what our Caps would do for them.

In November 1989, I met Bill Hansen from Swanson Health Products of Fargo, North Dakota at a health show in Minneapolis.

Bill had taken Power Caps and thought they would sell in the Swanson Health Catalog. We placed an ad for them in the January 1990 issue. The ad cost $1,200. The Heart Foods Company had no money, but I could pay for the ad with product. I couldn't imagine selling that many Power Caps.

We sold $7,700 in Power Caps with that ad.

In January 1990, Heart Foods began to become a real company. The sales from the Swanson Catalog and the capsule-filling machine changed everything. We moved into a new building for start-up companies in Minneapolis. It was in an old part of town that the city and some Native American people were rebuilding.

Sales in the Swanson Catalog rose every month. We offered Heart Food Caps and Thinking Caps. Both sold well. We made Tick Attack again that summer and it sold well, too.

The building we were in was new, well designed and well built, but it wasn't designed for us. Whenever we ground up those hot little African Birdseye Cayenne Peppers, acrid fumes permeated the building. They got into every office. Eyes burned. People choked. Meetings were disrupted. People were seen taking their telephones into the hallway, where they could breathe.

When we used Garlic or Ginger in a formula, the odor spread everywhere. The Valerian we used one day to make Happy Caps smelled so bad our neighbor thought there was a dead mouse in her office.

We closed all the air vents and sealed ourselves off from

the rest of the building, but that didn't help. It was too late. The building was saturated with herbs. We had to stop adding to the problem.

In early 1991, we moved into a defunct supermarket on a corner considered the toughest in town. Our parking lot got a fresh coat of broken glass every night. There were so many marked and unmarked police cars around, you couldn't find a place to park. We had shootings, stabbings, fights and arrests every day. The little black guy who swept the parking lot was shot in the head three times in the nearby park. I returned from the bank one morning, to find the door blocked by a woman with a knife in her chest. Life on the edge was never dull.

Our sales in the Swanson catalog continued to grow. In January 1991, sales broke $30,000, mostly in Power Caps, Heart Food Caps and Thinking Caps.

The Caps didn't sell very well in retail health food stores, because we didn't have enough money to buy national advertising. Most Americans didn't know much about Cayenne, just as I didn't in 1978.

Most important, I found that people who tried the Caps, tended to continue taking them. Cayenne works for me; obviously it was working for other people. I was more determined than ever to spread the word.

The FDA enters the picture

In April 1991, the U.S. Food and Drug Administration (FDA) ordered Swanson Health Products to stop selling our products in their catalog because they objected to the advertising. Other people could sell them, but not Swanson. They were specifically forbidden to sell Heart Food Caps "or anything similarly formulated."

The Heart Foods Company lost $14,000 in monthly sales because of the FDA's action. We kept operating, but we were actually dead in the water. Neither health food distributors nor catalog publishers would sell our Caps because they feared it might incur the FDA's wrath.

We had some other Cap sales and Tick Attack season was beginning, so we weren't entirely dead yet.

In July 1991, the FDA sent us a "Warning Letter" objecting to our ads, labels, names and literature. They also banned the sale of Night Caps for sleep and Gas Caps for nausea because they said only drugs could be sold for those purposes. I asked them about registering our products as drugs but they said that was impossible.

I answered the FDA "Warning Letter" with four letters of my own. I told them how we were complying with their letter and asking them what we could say about our Caps. I asked if we could relate the historical use of the herb over the centuries, how it was being used now in the rest of the world, what recognized herbalists said about it or data from documented clinical studies. They didn't answer.

In November 1991, the Environmental Protection Agency banned Tick Attack because it wasn't registered. Registration would take many years and cost millions, unless we added DEET to the formula, which we weren't willing to do. We used the money from Tick Attack sales in that last summer before the ban to buy a display and attend a couple of health food shows. We hoped health food stores, distributors and catalogs would sell our Caps. A few did, but most were afraid the FDA would attack them when they next attacked us.

Ironically, the Heart Foods Company was "left for dead" by the Health Food Industry, just as I was "left for dead" 13 years ago by the Medical Establishment.

The original ad published by Dick Quinn to promote Heart Foods.

"I believe that more than 90% of modern medicine could disappear from the face of the earth and the effect would be immediate and beneficial."

Robert Mendelsohn
Confessions of a Medical Heretic

7

FAREWELL TO
HEART FOODS

In early 1992, I resigned from the Heart Foods Company so I could tell you about Cayenne.

As part of a company that sells Cayenne, I couldn't tell you about it. The FDA would arrest me for breaking their circle of secrecy and telling the nasty truth.

They would charge me with medical fraud and shut down the Heart Foods Company, just when so many people have come to rely on its products.

I am a doctor with only one patient: myself. I don't diagnose, advise or prescribe for anyone else. I am a patient, like you are. I want you to have the same chance to live that I had.

When I discovered Cayenne in 1978, I was dying. Cayenne saved my life. It was almost miraculous. With the grace of God and His herbs, I was 56 years old on February 5, 1992. I feel great today, as I have since October 21, 1978. Cayenne has done that for me; maybe it will do it for you, too. But not if you don't know about it.

We are all at risk of a heart attack and we know it. Every day I meet people who have changed their life styles, hoping to live longer. TV ads sell foods with hope. Margarine becomes medicine in the frenzy to lower cholesterol and avoid the heart attack bullet that awaits so many of us. It hit me at 42; it hit my mother at 38.

For thirteen years, I have watched the concern about

heart attack grow, knowing I have the secret shield everyone is looking for.

I am determined to tell you how I beat heart disease, no matter what it costs me. I don't care what you do with the knowledge, I just want you to have it. As a human being, I am obligated to help you if I can. That's why I wrote this.

Good luck and good health. I hope you live forever.

8
THE FDA

The FDA has attacked natural medicines and the people who sell them for 40 years.

They cause as much financial and emotional damage as possible, hoping to bankrupt the people who make and sell herbs and other natural medicines that many people prefer to drugs. They don't want Americans to buy natural products unless drug companies profit. But natural sales grow, as drug sales slow, so the FDA attacks intensify.

The FDA is nonfeasant.

It fails to meet its obligation to protect our right to know all the medical options and choose our own health care.

The FDA is malfeasant. As a regulatory agency, it must fairly oversee and assist the businesses it regulates, helping them to prosper. But the FDA maliciously attacks the natural health industry it is supposed to help. To promote drug sales, the FDA conducts a relentless campaign of industrial genocide. The FDA is a crooked cop.

The FDA has a conflict of interest.

The FDA is supposed to protect us, but they protect the drug companies from us, to our detriment. Their allegiance is to the medical establishment, not to the People.

The FDA must be fired.

We the People need an agency that will protect our right to choose our own health care, as the U.S. Constitution guarantees.

A new regulator must be appointed immediately, to assure free access to healthful natural alternatives to drugs.

Empower the U.S. Department of Agriculture to regulate all herbs, vitamins and other food medicines.

Give the People a free choice; they'll decide what to do.

Pharmacology is the science of drugs. The name comes from an ancient Greek word for poison.

9
LETTERS FROM THE HEART

"Ask the man who owns one."
Packard Automobile Ad

These are unsolicited letters from people who have discovered that herbs help them live longer, healthier lives. They depend on the herbs that the FDA wants to outlaw.

These people and all people have the right to choose and legally buy the medicines they decide to take for their own health and happiness. It is constitutionally guaranteed to every American. No one has the authority to take that right away, as the FDA wants to do.

To Whom it May Concern —
Thank you — Sure like
Power Caps — even improved
my eyesight —
Thanks again —

AUGUST 21, 1991

MR. RICHARD QUINN
PRESIDENT
THE HEART FOODS COMPANY
1913 CHICAGO AVENUE SOUTH
MINNEAPOLIS, MN 55404

DEAR MR. QUINN:

IN 1941, WHEN I WAS A FRESHMAN IN HIGH SCHOOL, I
SPENT TEN WEEKS IN ST FRANCIS HOSPITAL IN GRINNELL,
IOWA WITH PNEUMONIA. AFTER I WAS FINALLY DISCHARGED
FROM THE HOSPITAL I LEARNED THAT I HAD PERMANENT
LUNG DAMAGE FROM THE ILLNESS. THIS WAS CALLED PLEURISY
AND I HAVE HAD PAIN FROM THIS EVERY DAY FOR THE PAST
49 YEARS, UNTIL I WAS INTRODUCED TO YOUR POWER CAPS
A FEW MONTHS AGO. I CURRENTLY TAKE 3-4 CAPSULES
PER DAY AND HAVE HAD NO PAIN SINCE I HAVE BEEN USING
THE POWER CAPS. I ALSO NOTICE THAT I HAVE MUCH MORE
STRENGTH AND ENERGY THAN I USED TO HAVE AND CAN WORK
RINGS AROUND THE YOUNGER GENERATION AT THE HEALTH
CLUB WHERE I WORK OUT FOUR TIMES A WEEK.

THANK YOU FOR IMPROVING MY QUALITY OF LIFE, IT'S
GREAT!

SINCERELY,

████████████████████████████████████

Heart Foods
Box 5420   Sept. 23, 1991
Minneapolis, Mn.

Gentlemen:

We have been buying "Heart Caps" from Swanson
Health Products. Recently they informed us that
they had discontinued this line.

My husband depends on these capsules, so
I am writing you to inquire if we can get
them directly from you.

An early reply will be appreciated.

Thank You,

████████████████████████████████

Shelby, Mi. 49455

Brooklyn New York   May 12, 1991

Dear Mr. Richard Quinn!

I am writing to you to tell that I bought your heart food for my heart condition and can not thank you enough for saving my life. I am sixty two years old and have blocked arteries with pain in my heart every day. I do not wish to go in for surgery as I do not have the money to pay for this expensive operation. So I am taking your heart food and given up taking nitroglycerin tablets to stop the pain in my heart. I would appreciate it very much if you could be so kind to add another fine herb for the heart called motherwort to your heart food as it is one of the finest herbs for the heart besides Hawthorne Berries. But it must be 100% organically grown with no pesticides used to grow this wonderful herb. Also can you tell me if the soya lecithin you use in your heart food contains any soy oil as this can cause more blockage in my arteries and cause me to have a heart attack. Thanking you always for saving my life I will continue to buy your heart food than have surgery which is dangerous and unsuccessful in curing heart disease.

                    Yours in health

Memphis Tn. 38122
Aug. 3, 1991

The Heart Food Co.
Dear Sir,

I do appreciate you sending them, I was frantic when Swanson returning my check saying they could no longer sell them. In desperation I took a chance from the add on the bottle. Am so glad I did. Swanson is so nice to do business with and they carry other product I use. Thanks for sending them to me.

Nov. 17, 1990.

Sir:
I have been using 450mg cayenne pepper capsules for nocturnal leg cramps. It helped, but was not completely effective.

After seeing Heart Foods mentioned in Channel 6, I tried their power caps. What a revelation and improvement. The increased potency, plus giner and hawthorn, has not only eliminated my nocturnal leg cramps, but in addition, has given me so much energy that I do not need these mid-day naps. It has also eliminated my frequent headaches.

At 80 years of age, I welcome this quality life and highly recommend power caps to everyone.

Wed. June 5th, 1991

Dear Mr. Quinn,

In 1983 I suffere a bad heart attack but refused to go to the hospital on the grounds that I was too sick and might not survive medical mistreatment such as you had. I took about a 100 capsules, tablets etc. each day. At times I had to resort to a prescription pill to releave chest pain. I finally recovered pretty well but not 100%. Then I found a doctor who gave Chelation therapy. It took 20 treatments and a six month lay off back for another 10 treatments. I will be 70 years old if I last till Sept 15th. Thur May 30th I had another heart attack. I had been Square DAncing about five nites a week but the weather in chicago was hot as Hell and the churches where we dance are rarely air conditioned so I guess I just over did it.

This is where Heart Food comes in. I was confined to a lazy boy chair for two days and went back to my heart pain pills. They didn.t work. Perhaps they were just too cold. I used other methods to releave the pain but was dam scared. I remembered that I purchased your Heart Food and Power Caps but found them much too hot. I felt like my stomach was on fire. My mistake was I took both at the same time. I needed help so I just tried one capsule with cold (not ice water) and about an hour later I took the Power Cap,to my pleasant supprise there was no discomfort. I began to take three Heart Food Caps and three Energy Caps. Today is WEd. June 5th and I can't tell you the improvement I have experienced. I am able to drive mky car and do all my errands. There is still a great deal of weakness and there will be no square dancing for a while but so far I am pain free and able to get around. It was not the case in 1983. I plan to use Heart Food and Power Caps excusively. Will you please send me all information you might have on your products. I would like to introduce them to my patients and friends. Please include a price list. Thankyou for a great product.

sincerely,

    ____ Gorham DN-ND

P.S. Any product that seems to be as effective as yours has to come
     under the thumb of the Damnable FDA. Enclosed is a couple of
articles you might be interested in if you are not already aware of this
problem.

Gentlemen:

We have been taking heart food and have found it very beneficial. However, Swanson Health Products tells us it is no longer available by action of the FDA.

Is there any way or place — such as Canada that this would be available? Please advise.

Yours truly

Austin, MN.

NOTICE!

**SWANSON HEALTH PRODUCTS
NO LONGER OFFERS DDS
ACIDOPHILUS, ESTEEM
CARDIO LIFE OR HEART FOOD &
POWER CAPS AS LISTED
ON OUR MAIL ORDER ENVELOPES.
WE APOLOGIZE FOR ANY
INCONVENIENCE THIS MAY HAVE
CAUSED YOU.**

To Mr. Richard Quinn, Pres.

Ave been Buying my heart food Products for the past three years from swansons, now I can't get them. What should I do, can you help me?

Thank you,
John Steigerwald

P.S.
Im 65 Yrs. old. and I need these Products.

Hermitage P a
16148

Heart Foods:
Box 54120
Minneapolis MN. 55454-4

Dear Sirs:
Kindly inform me If I may Order Heart Foods From your Company. I have been Ordering From Swanson but They have discontinued it. my daughter Who is 55 years Old had a big heart attack at the Hospital Where she worked and Was misdiagnosed as a Pinched Nerve so When finally diagnosed she had inforcted and extended her MI. The Drs at Pittsburg Pa sent her home To die. She Was incurable and was a Diabetic. They gave her 6 Months To live That was in 1987. When I got her home I Put her on Heart Food and that was 3 years ago. She has now Gone back to Work as a R N. Pleasify we can get this heart Food Fro you I will be eternally greatful.

Thank you

Memphis Tenn 38122
July 21 1991

Heart Foods
Dear Sir
    Am writing you regarding
your Heart food product.
I have been getting it through
Swanson. Recently I ordered
2 - 60 count bottles and they
returned my check saying
they could no longer sell it
    I am sorry I can't get it
any more It had helped
me so much I was dizzy
and staggering since I began
taking it I don't have those
spells so I am writing to you
to ask you to please let them
continue to sell them or let me
buy them direct through you
    Please let me hear from
you I don't want to get back like I
Was.
        Thank you

Dear Sir,   10-31-91

I am very please
with your Heart Food
I had a heart attack
Feb 3, 198 and have had
a Dull pains across my
back for 14 years and
since taking your Heart
Food and Power Caps.
I have no more pain
Thanks,
You have come out with
another product I think
about brain power but I
can't find a supplyer

Please inform me
as who handles these
products for your
Company
Thanks

79

Chicago 60630
Feb 29. 1992

Dear Mr Gunn.

I have been using your heart pills, for several months now. I am writing to thank you, for making them. I have a heart blockage. The artery leading to the heart is about 40 per cent blocked. the dr said was serious. He prescribed capiton. I didn'feel any change.
So. one day I read your add for Heart pills. So I ordered 2 Bottles. After the first day I could feel such a change. my chest head seemed so clogged I felt awful. your pills gave a clear head, chest. I could feel the air when I would breath so wonderful. So I will continue taking them. I take four pills a day. I tried taking three times a day. It caused such a heart-burn. Sould I trey taking them 3 times a day? all I can say they are wonderful.

Thank you.

Before recieving the Healthy Times My Husband was Taking Enduron and Nitro. We ordered the Cayenne Pepper And that is all he takes now. Today Doctor told him "You Are getting Healther every day, I will see you one more time then you probably wont have to come back again unless you get sick." No more High Priced Medicine for him. His Blood Pressure is Normal his Cholesterol is normal and he feels good. 76 years old has a beautiful garden and works in it every day even When the Temp is 100 and over.

Thank You so Much

ROBERT F. QUINN

HEALTH FOODS

NORTH EDWARDS, CA
93523

DEAR SIR:

I REIORDERED YOU EXCELLENT HEART
FOOD PRODUCT WHICH REALLY GAVE ME
FANTASTIC RESULTS - IN FACT, IT FUNCTIONS
SO GOOD I WOULDN'T KNOW I HAD A
HEART. - I ENCLOSED THE LETTER
FROM SWANSON CONCERNING YOUR FINE
PRODUCT - I DONT UNDERSTAND THIER
ATTITUDE ABOUT SUCH A FINE HERB
FOOD. - AS THERE ARE NO SIDE EFFECTS,
FROM ITS DAILY USE, NONE AT ALL.

PLEASE ADVISE ME IF I CAN GET
HEART FOOD, AND POWER CAPS FROM
YOU - ALSO IF YOU HAVE TO DISPOSE OF
YOUR CURRENT STOCK, IM READY TO BUY
ON A REGULAR BASIS! your

Mr. Richard F. Quinn
1433 E. Franklin St.
Minneapolis, Minn.   55404

Pineland, Florida
33945

October 12, 1990

Dear Sir:

    I came across your "Power Cap" quite by accident
and decided to try to test them on myself as an experiment to determine their effectiveness on circulation. I
can truly say that they are an answer to anyone suffering from this. I highly recommend them.

    My only concern is that like a lot of health pro-
ducts they may go off the market some day and become lost
to those who have used them. I trust you will continue
to offer them for a long time.

                        Sincerely yours,

Sept - 14-91

Dear Richard,

I am convinced! Your "Heart Foods" capsules truly work! Being around the health food industry vis-a-vis my family all my life I've always taken herbs and vitamins sporatically. However, after meeting you and Susan. I decided to try your product and it is great! I feel better, I've lost weight, my confidence has excelled beyond my wildest imagination, I sleep better. I am fan for life with "Heart Food".

Nov 17, 1991

Heart Foods
Richard Quinn.

Dear Richard,

First off, I want to tell you how much
we appreciate your products which we have
been using ever since we read your articles
in Swanson's Health Shopper.

But we cannot understand why Mr.
Swanson does not carry your products in
his catalog any longer. He sent out a note
with something about your products on his
envelopes attached to the order blank.

I feel bad about that because Dr. Swanson
has his products on every envelope.

And now I have used our last Power cap
and my husband is recuperating from a 2 month
illness and he used the power Caps to improve
his circulation. He still has those dizzy
spells, and it worries me so much.

Would you please tell me where I may
purchase the products which you have?
I mean all of them.

I have recommended the Power Caps to
several people; now they will not be able
to get them from Swansons either.

Please keep me.

Sincerely

Roland, Okla. 74954

9-11-91
Lowellville
Ohio 44436

Richard F. Quinn,

I am writing in regard to your Heart Food Caps. I ordered a few times from Swanson Health Products, but now they tell me they are not allowed to sell them because of advertising problems. "Where oh where" can I get them? The health food stores in my area do not sell them. I honestly think they did me some good.

My husband had quadruple by-pass surgery in May 1990. I was giving them to him and I was taking them for high blood pressure and high cholestrol.

Maybe the FDA thinks its cheaper to have surgery.

Also how do the other people who advertise in Swanson's & get away with it? People like Susser & Jason & others

July 11, 1991

Mr. Quinn —

My husband and I were very disappointed when we tried to order your Heart Foods from Swansons and were told they were no longer able to handle your products.

Thank heavens, the young lady who answered the phone gave us the telephone number of your company!

My husband is 83 years old and has a "heart problem".

I had read the "propaganda" about your Heart Food and Pep Pills in Swanson's literature and sent for them.

I had figured they wouldn't hurt him, but I didn't honestly expect his body to react as quickly as it did. He really felt great within 30 minutes time.

I honestly don't remember reading any claims which Swanson's made which your literature doesn't claim, but, I know the F.D.I is sometimes inclined to make some "mysterious" rulings.

In any event, I'm glad we found you, again.

86

10
PRESCRIPTIONS FOR MYSELF

I have acted as my own doctor since discovering herbs in 1978 and I have done a pretty good job. When I get ill, I first try to deal with it myself, then go to a chiropractor or naturopathic doctor. If I had appendicitis, I'd probably go to the hospital and have it taken out—but not without misgivings.

I am a physician, if only for myself, so I must follow the oath of Hippocrates and "do no harm" to my patient. Since herbal medicine is the safest, most effective medicine for me, I try that first. There are herbs for everything.

I grew up with drugs. Everybody smoked and drank in 1950. The doctor's drugs and surgery were good, because his intentions were good. People still trusted.

I didn't realize how harmful drugs are until I saw their devastating effects on me and my friends.

I didn't realize how dangerous and debilitating surgery can be until I had it. Drugs and surgery do have their place. If I had a car accident or were at war, I would want access to them. There are many drug successes, but drugs are used even when they don't work.

As patients, you and I must have access to all treatments available, so we can be sure to find the best treatment for ourselves. Not the most profitable or most politically approved treatment, but the very best way to regain and maintain our health and happiness.

It's too bad we can't trust. We can't believe what the doctor tells us, because he often doesn't know what's right. We can't believe drug companies, because they care only about profits and exhibit limitless greed. We can't trust the need for surgery because referring doctors get paid for every "sale." We can't trust the FDA to protect us because they work for the other side. We just pay the bill.

It's too bad, but we're on our own.

I have had no medical training and, until my own heart attack, I wasn't interested. But I am interested now. I don't give advice — I have no idea what treatment is best for you. I want you to know your options, as I know mine. I hope you'll look further and read books by other writers with other opinions. I can only tell you what I do for myself.

Take charge of your health. Make your own decisions. You're worth saving.

How I get energy and feel good every day

I take four capsules of Cayenne every morning giving me a bit more than one gram. I take a blend of 100,000 heat unit Cayenne from Africa and India. Cayenne is nature's most powerful stimulant. It gives me terrific energy that lasts hours. Most people could get by on one or two Cayenne capsules.

Cayenne from the grocery store has about 5,000 heat units of potency, but it gave me energy when I needed it most. Health stores sell 40,000 heat unit Cayenne and cooperative grocery stores often sell 60,000 to 80,000 h.u. Cayenne.

Pick your power. It all works.

How I prevent tiredness

Whenever I feel myself getting tired, I take more Cayenne and get a nice lift in about 10 minutes. It works faster if I mix the Cayenne with tomato or grape juice and drink it.

Cayenne capsules can upset your stomach, but bread,

crackers or a roll put the fire out fast. Cream and ice cream work, too.

I never take it with hot coffee.

Caffeine stimulates by shutting down your arteries while Cayenne opens them wider. Taken together they make me feel sick and tired.

How I deal with tension and stress after work

I used to come home from work every day with a burning stiffness in my neck and shoulders. I thought it was from typing. I tried massage and exercise, but couldn't get rid of it.

One day I read the herb Valerian was supposed to be very relaxing, so I bought some and took it after work. In a few minutes my stiff, burning neck and shoulder muscles relaxed and the pain disappeared.

After seeing how well Valerian relaxed my tension-caused muscle pain, I made a formulation for stress that combined Valerian with Cayenne and Catnip, the safe herbal tranquilizer, but straight Valerian will do the job.

My diet

I eat what I like and don't worry about it. Cayenne keeps my arteries clean and helps me control my weight by raising my metabolism.

Exercise

Low impact exercise is best for me. I am not trying to build muscle, I'm just doing rust control. Calisthenics bore me, but I like to ride a bike. In the summer, I often ride around for hours; in winter I ride an exercycle while reading the newspaper.

For several years after my bypass I got little or no exercise, but I now see its importance.

How I avoid colds and flu

Cayenne and Garlic, which I take every day, seem to kill most of the bugs that cause colds and flu. In fact, I never get the flu, but I do sometimes get a cold. When I feel a cold coming on, I take Goldenseal, the remarkable antibiotic herb, with Cayenne.

I also take vitamin C for a cold, as recommended by Linus Pauling, the Nobel Prize winning chemist. I take up to 50,000 mgs. of vitamin C on the first day of a cold, 25,000 mg. on the second day and as needed thereafter. It stops my cold symptoms fast. Vitamin C gives some people an upset stomach or even diarrhea, but it doesn't bother me.

How I treat diarrhea

Herbs work quickly and safely for diarrhea. I have found 1/2 teaspoon of ground Nutmeg taken several times a day can stop diarrhea.

I often mix the Nutmeg with Slippery Elm Bark and Red Raspberry Leaves for even faster action.

Constipation hasn't been a problem...

Many, many herbs have a laxative action, but I can't recommend any. I take so much Cayenne, I am never constipated.

Senna, Cascara Sagrada, Turkey Rhubarb, Aloe Vera and Psyllium are effective. Some laxative herbs may lead to habitual use or should be avoided during pregnancy; some are entirely safe. Be sure to read the label before you use any laxative.

How I treat hemorrhoids

I use the classic home remedy for hemorrhoids: a slice of raw potato and liquid vitamin E. Cayenne works great to stop itching and bleeding fast, and promotes healing. But it does burn for a few minutes. Nothing is free.

How I treat swollen glands

I have had a tendency to get very painful swollen glands in my neck since my tonsils were taken out as a child. For years, I suffered through the pain, but now I stop it fast with a combination of Golden Seal Root, Myrrh, Hyssop, White Willow Bark and Saw Palmetto, the herb for glands.

I take six to ten capsules daily until well.

What I use instead of aspirin

I use White Willow Bark, called "nature's aspirin" because it contains so much salicin, aspirin's main ingredient. Safer than aspirin, it doesn't cause kidney failure like Ibupropen or fatal overdose.

Herbs I use instead of antibiotic drugs

Hyssop is called "nature's penicillin" because of the mold on its leaves. Golden Seal Root, Burdock Root, Garlic, Chaparral, Cayenne, Comfrey, Echinacea and Myrrh all contain unique anti-biotic, anti-bacterial and anti-viral agents I have used to treat infection and illness. I take Garlic and Cayenne every day and use Golden Seal, Myrrh, Chaparral and Burdock for something special, like a sore throat.

I use Aloe for cuts and burns

When I cut or burn myself, I cover it with a bandage made of Aloe Vera. I cut a frond from the plant, open it up and put the fleshy inside against the wound. Tape it in place and leave it on overnight. The next morning, the wound will be sealed and the Aloe will have turned black.

It's important to get the heat out of burns before applying Aloe. I soak the burn in ice water until all the heat is out and there is no pain when dry, then apply Aloe.

How I stop bleeding and minor infection

I have found that Cayenne stops bleeding on contact, but it can sting. I once stopped serious bleeding instantly with ordinary Cayenne. I use it when I cut myself shaving.

I also use Cayenne to kill minor infections from cuts and scrapes.

How I strengthen my immune system

Garlic and Cayenne contain anti-biotics and disinfectants that protect against illness and provide needed nutrition. Drugs provide no nutrition. Herbalists say Kelp, Licorice, and Echinacea aid the immune system, too.

How I avoid leg cramps

Circulation is the key to avoiding leg cramps and Cayenne is the key to circulation. Prickly Ash, Cinchona (also called Peruvian Bark) and Gingko Biloba stimulate circulation in the legs.

How I have avoided rheumatism and arthritis

Arthritis and rheumatism are not diseases, they are symptoms, and can have many causes.

Cayenne brings blood to my joints and muscles, so they stay warm and flexible. It's especially helpful when I have to drive a long distance or spend hours sitting and cannot walk to stimulate circulation in my legs and feet. Burdock is a joint-warming antibiotic herb for arthritis, but I have never needed it. (Please see Gout below.)

How I deal with gout

I once thought only lazy old men get gout. I didn't realize I was wrong until I got it myself.

The herb Queen of the Meadow (also called Gravelroot) stops my gout fast. I took six to ten capsules per day and it improved immediately. In a couple of days, it was gone.

Next time I have gout, I'll eat six to ten cherries (canned or fresh) every day until it's gone. The cherries are supposed to work quickly and they're guaranteed to taste good.

How I keep my hands and feet warm

Cayenne is a circulatory stimulant that keeps my hands and feet warm. I have also sprinkled some Cayenne in my stockings as extra protection on especially cold Winter days in Minnesota.

How I deal with headaches

Cerebral circulation is my key to headache prevention, so I take Cayenne and Gotu Kola daily. Gotu Kola is the mental stimulant and anti-aging herb from India; Cayenne is the powerful circulatory stimulant. Together, they're the best headache medicine I have found.

If I ever get a migraine headache, I'll see if the herbs Feverfew and Wood Betony stop it.

How I avoid insomnia and sleep well

There are many sleep herbs, but a combination of Valerian, Passion Flower and Skullcap works for me. These herbs are safe, addiction-free and do not cause a hangover. Passion Flower is the most popular sleep herb in Europe.

Hops is a safe, effective sleep herb which I don't take because it can cause heart pain. To make a "hops pillow," put hops leaves into a bag and tuck it under your pillow, where you will inhale the aroma. It works for insomnia.

How I maintain a healthy sex life

Many men can't get an erection because of poor circulation and this, certainly, causes embarrassment and attitude problems. People with low energy are often depressed — another factor affecting their sex lives. Blood pressure drugs, beta blockers and other drugs often cause impotence and depression.

I find that Cayenne boosts my circulation, so I can get the blood where I need it, when I need it. Strong circulation makes everything work better.

I also sometimes take Saw Palmetto, the herb for the glands, and Damiana, the genital herb, for sexual health.

How I avoid prostate problems

Herbalists recommend Cayenne for prostate, so that's probably why I never have had any problems. Kelp and Saw Palmetto is also prescribed for a healthy prostate. Saw Palmetto, a berry from the Palmetto palm, acts on the enlarged prostate to reduce inflamation, pain and swelling. Parsley eases urination.

How I keep my skin healthy

Cayenne is a "peripheral circulatory stimulant" which brings blood and nutrition to the skin, keeping it healthy.

Skin is high in cholesterol and needs a stable supply of blood and oxygen. Tobacco smokers have restricted peripheral circulation, so their skin is less healthy. Cayenne is said to reduce the tendency to wrinkle and keep skin smooth and youthful longer. Like Gotu Kola, Cayenne is an anti-aging herb. Both are good for the skin.

How I lower my cholesterol and clean my arteries

I take Cayenne, Garlic, Onion and Ginger to keep the walls of my arteries clean and help my body rid itself of cholesterol.

Cayenne causes my liver to produce less cholesterol. The combination of Ginger, Garlic and Onion has been shown in controlled studies to lower cholesterol as efficiently as drugs, with no liver damage or other side effects.

Side effects of Cholesterol-lowering drugs can be far more serious than high cholesterol.

How I prevent irregular heartbeat

When I got very tired, my heart used to run irregularly and bang against my chest so hard I could see my shirt move.

Valerian strengthens my heart and smoothes the heartbeat, no matter how tired I am. I take two or three capsules of Valerian to do the job. It can also be blended with Passion Flower, the sleep herb that's also good for the heart.

How I prevent atrial fibrillation

Herbalists recommend Cayenne and Valerian to prevent fibrillation or stop it once it has started. It works so well for me I made a formulation that combines Cayenne and Valerian with Catnip, a stomach settling herbal tranquilizer.

Herbalists also recommend Motherwort Herb to prevent and treat palpitations and fibrillation, but I have never tried it. It's supposed to be especially good for women.

How I regulate my blood pressure

The most recommended herbal combination to lower blood pressure is Cayenne and Garlic. Valerian is also said to lower blood pressure. I take all three every day because I have a history of high blood pressure.

Herbalists also recommend Celery Seed, Hawthorn, Passion Flower, Skullcap, Valerian, Primrose, Barberry, Don Quai, Kelp, Siberian Genseng, Blue and Black Cohosh, Wild Yam Root, and Gotu Kola to lower blood pressure.

Herbs such as Passion Flower and Valerian work by reducing stress-caused tension, while Cayenne and Garlic open circulatory channels and cleanse internal organs so blood flows more freely and pressure goes down.

According to a study at Boston's Beth Israel Hospital and the Washington Hospital Center, fish oil high in Omega-3 lowers blood pressure.

For low blood pressure Brigham Tea, Dandelion and Parsley can be used. Cayenne and Hawthorn normalize blood pressure that's too high or low.

Drugs suppress blood pressure without regard to its cause and often result in other medical problems such as kidney damage, depression and impotence. Some drugs actually induce a heart attack and cause chemical dependence, so you can't stop taking them.

Herbs treat the cause of high blood pressure and provide nutrition for whole body health. Drugs provide no nutrition.

Note: Herbs lower blood pressure naturally, so you may have to reduce dosage of blood pressure drugs.

How I prevent angina

The herb said to prevent angina pectoris is Hawthorn. I take it every day.

Angina Pectoris is a sharp pain, usually in one or both arms, in the chest, shoulder or back. It occurs when a chamber of the heart doesn't get enough blood because of blood clots or other obstructions. Although angina is not harmful in itself, it is an ominous sign of impending heart attack.

The drug nitroglycerine stops angina pain, but does nothing to correct the cause or prevent future angina. Medical studies show implants that secrete nitroglycerine to prevent angina work for only a short time.

How I avoid a heart attack

I take Cayenne and Garlic first thing every morning to make a heart attack less likely.

Most heart attacks occur in the morning, when the arteries are constricted because of stress, caffeine and other factors.

Cayenne and Garlic open the arteries, stimulate the heart and dissolve blood clots that cause 95% of all heart attacks.

How I would stop a heart attack in progress

Dr. John Christopher showed a heart attack can be stopped by putting Cayenne tea under the tongue or having the patient drink it. Just stir up some Cayenne and warm water.

Capsules, Herbs and other needs...

I take herbs in capsules because it's faster and easier. I can just swallow some capsules of Cayenne every morning and I'm set. But some people can't swallow capsules or can't get them where they live. There are other ways to do it.

I often mix a half or full teaspoon of Cayenne into ice cold tomato juice and drink it down. If I let the mixture stand around, it gets incredibly hot as the oily capsaiacin leeches into the juice. To beat the heat, chugalug. It will give you a shot you'll feel now.

Other herbs can be taken the same way; Garlic, Onion and Hawthorn, for example.

Bread Capsules

Another alternative is to make bread capsules. Just tear the center out of a piece of fresh bread, or fresh roll. Flatten it out; dampen, if necessary. Cut 1 or 2 inch squares or circles — whatever size you like — and roll up your herbs inside like making a buritto. Take them with a lot of water or chew them up. The bread makes the herb easier to take.

Herbs...

You can buy Cayenne in any food or health store. Though culinary Cayenne is low powered at 5,000 heat units, I got plenty of energy from it when I first took Cayenne in 1978.

You can buy 40,000 heat unit Cayenne in capsules. Good brands include Nature's Herbs, Nature's Way and Solaray. Nature's Way also sells bulk Cayenne in 1/4 lb. packages. Heart Foods uses a 100,000 heat unit Cayenne blend in its products.

Bulk Cayenne sold in some food and health stores as "Hot Cayenne," can have 80,000 to 90,000 heat units.

My heat unit ratings

Canned Cayenne from grocery store . . . . 5,000 h.u.
Tabasco Cayenne, Jalopenos . . . . 20-30,000 h.u.
Chinese Cayenne for herbalists . . . . 40,000 h.u.
Ghoa Cayenne from Bombay . . . . 90,000 h.u.
African Birdseye Cayenne . . . . 135-150,000 h.u.
Habanero Pepper . . . . 200-300,000 h.u.

How I get my vitamins and minerals

There are many natural vitamins and minerals in herbs. Cayenne is high in vitamin C, vitamin A (beta carotene) and zinc. Garlic is high in Chromium, Phosphorus, Selenium and Thiamine. Ginger has lots of Manganese and Potassium. Gotu Kola has Magnesium and vitamin A.

Herbs have "naturally occurring" vitamins and minerals, which are easy for your body to identify and use. Synthetic vitamins and minerals are often wasted because they can not be identified and used by the body.

Juicing and Vegetarian Nutrition

I have read the books of Dr. N.W. Walker, heard The "Juice Man" and tried juicing myself. It seems an ideal health practice, especially for cleansing. Juicing has shown considerable success against cancer.

We have a juicer and we use it.

Many highly respected nutritionists espouse a vegetarian diet for everyone and show the harm done by meat, milk, eggs and other things we have always eaten. I'm sure vegetarianism is right for many people.

There are herbs for cancer, diabetes, TB, AIDS, Alzheimer's and every other disease, but I haven't needed them so far. You can read about them in many good books including:

Herbally Yours by Penny C. Royal
Killing Cancer by Sir Jason Winters
The Scientific Validation of Herbal Medicine
    by Daniel B. Mowry
School of Natural Healing by Dr. John Christopher
Back to Eden by Jethro Kloss
Planetary Herbalogy by Michael Tierra

Some sources...

Frontier Herbal Co-op—herbs & supplies 1-800-669-3275
Cayenne Trading Co.—Quinn's Blend formulas 1-800-641-6802
Nature's Herbs—mfgr. herbs & formulas 1-800-437-2257
Home Health—mail order health products ... 1-800-284-9123
L&H Vitamins—mail order health catalog.... 1-800-221-1152
Swanson Health Products—mail order catalog 1-800-437-4148
Nature's Way—mfgr. herbs & formulas 1-800-926-8883

"Leave your drugs in the chemist's pot if you can heal the patient with food."

Hippocrates, the Father of Medicine

PART II

HERBS FOR THE HEART

by Shannon Quinn

"The Lord has created medicines from the earth, and a sensible man will not disparage them. There is no end to the works of the Lord, who spreads health all over the world."

CAYENNE *(Capsicum Annum)*

11
CAYENNE

Cayenne *(latin name: Capsicum annum; family: Solanaceae)* has been used since the beginning of history in South and Central America as a culinary and medicinal herb. Cayenne comes from the fruit of the red pepper plant. This bright red fruit grows in warm tropical climates on small perennial shrubs that bloom with white flowers in late summer. Cayenne pepper is a fruit, much like a tomato.

Varieties of Cayenne are cultivated all over the world. The strength and medicinal value range from the most powerful pepper grown in Sierra Leone, Africa to the mild paprika enjoyed in Hungary.

Cayenne, which takes its name from the Greek word meaning "to bite," was introduced to Europe by Christopher Columbus. Legend has it that Columbus discovered the pungent pepper growing on an island off French Guiana later called Devil's Island.

Although there is evidence that Cayenne had been cultivated in South America and Africa for centuries, the rest of the world had to wait for their first taste until Columbus returned home in 1493. No reference to Cayenne has been found in ancient Chinese, Greek, Hebrew, Latin or Sanskrit.

One of the most effective stimulants, Cayenne targets the digestive and the circulatory system primarily. Cayenne regulates blood pressure, strengthens the pulse, feeds the heart, lowers cholesterol, thins the blood, cleanses the circulatory system, heals ulcers, stops hemorrhaging, speeds healing of wounds, rebuilds damaged tissue, eases congestion, aids digestion, regulates elimination, relieves arthritis and rheumatism, prevents the spread of infection and numbs pain.

Cayenne stimulates every system and cell of the body. Cayenne has been valued around the world for its uses as a stimulant, astringent, antispasmodic, circulatory tonic, antidepressant and antibacterial agent. In addition, Cayenne acts as a diaphoretic to induce sweating, a rubefacient to increase circulation at the skin's surface and a carminative to help prevent and eliminate gas.

Used as a condiment, Cayenne aids digestion and soothes intestinal ailments by stimulating the stomach to produce mucous. In China, the pungent pepper has been used to stimulate the appetite and promote the flow of saliva which, in turn, aids digestion.

In the circulatory system, Cayenne helps the arteries, veins and capillaries regain the elasticity of youth by feeding the cell structure. Cayenne helps equalize circulation by regulating the flow of blood from the head to the feet. Cayenne strengthens the pulse by increasing the power, not the frequency. Generally, Cayenne boosts overall health of the entire cardiovascular system.

Cayenne's ability to help lower cholesterol was first noticed during a routine experiment at the Central Food Technological Research Institute in Mysore, India. When scientists at the institute added Cayenne to the high cholesterol diet the test animals were being fed, there was not the usual rise in serum and liver cholesterol. Instead, the cholesterol was being excreted. Cayenne prevented the absorbtion of cholesterol.

Further studies showed that diet plays an integral part in Cayenne's ability to help the body shed excess cholesterol. Cayenne was unable to influence cholesterol intake when the diet contained little protein. With enough protein in the diet, Cayenne was able to inhibit cholesterol absorption significantly.

In addition to helping prevent the build-up of cholesterol which can narrow the veins and arteries, Cayenne also helps thin the blood and prevent blood clots that can clog the arteries and cause heart attack and stroke. Ingesting Cayenne stimulates the body's fibrinolytic system helping prevent clots from forming and dissolving clots that had already formed, according to a study performed at Siriraj Hospital in Bangkok, Thailand.

The surge in fibrinolytic activity lasted for up to 30 minutes after the Cayenne was eaten. The temporary nature of this boost in the function of the fibrinolytic system is important because if it were prolonged it could lead to problems such as excessive bleeding.

Daily doses of Cayenne keep the fibrinolytic system operating efficiently. Perhaps this is why natives living in New Guinea, Africa, Korea, India and Thailand have a lower instance of thrombolic disease and greater fibrinolytic activity than caucasians living in the same areas who do not make Cayenne a part of their daily diet.

In more ways than any other herb, Cayenne gets the blood moving. Touted as "the purest and most certain stimulant known to man," Cayenne is considered to be one of the best crisis herbs. By helping the circulatory system operate more efficiently, the snappy red pepper boosts the energy level and eases the damaging effects of stress on the body.

A series of tests performed on animals demonstrated Cayenne's stimulating effects to be immediate but transient. Experimental Psychologist Daniel Mowrey used rats in a stress test of Cayenne. The rats were first trained to jump a barrier in order to avoid a mild shock to their feet. The animals were then dropped into a container of water and forced to swim for several minutes. Exhausted, the rats were put back in the original test chamber to see if they could still leap over the barrier. Mowry found that the rats who were given Cayenne were more able to overcome their fatigue and jump the barrier than their rodent counterparts.

To test speed as well as stamina, Mowry performed another experiment in which the rats were trained to climb a pole to reach the sugar water they craved. According to Mowry, the rats on the Cayenne diet climbed the pole much more rapidly than the others.

In experiments on human subjects at the University of

Dusseldorf, Cayenne was found to increase the patient's ability to concentrate. The stimulant and anti-fatigue effects of Cayenne were found to be immediate, temporary and harmless.

By increasing the circulation of the blood to peripheral tissues throughout the body, Cayenne helps deliver necessary nutrients to inflamed and infected areas. Studies show that the nutrients in food ingested with Cayenne are assimulated faster and more easily.

The herb itself contains many nutrients essential to the health of the circulatory system including alpha-tocopherols, vitamin C and minerals. Cayenne also contains a high amount of vitamin A (beta-carotene) which aids in healing ulcers. The redder the Cayenne pepper, the more vitamin A it contains. Paprika, the mildest Cayenne, has the highest vitamin C content of all. Cayenne, the vibrant red fruit bursting with heat and energy, holds more vitamin C and beta-carotene than any other plant in the garden.

Cayenne's high mineral content, including sulphur, iron, calcium, magnesium and phosphorus, makes it an effective treatment for diabetes, gas, arthritis, pancreatic and throat disorders. The high vitamin C content of the fruit helps target colds, while the tremendous amount of beta-carotene helps speed the healing of ulcers.

One of the most remarkable qualities of Cayenne is its ability to act as a catalyst. Cayenne intensifies the beneficial effects of other herbs by ensuring speedy and thorough distribution of the herb's active components to the important functional centers of the body such as those responsible for metabolism, data transmission, cellular respiration and neural hormonal activity.

A little bit of Cayenne goes a long way. Since just a small quantity of Cayenne can dramatically increase the efficiency of most herbs, this catalyst herb is added to nearly every herbal combination available.

Added to Garlic, for example, Cayenne speeds up the antibiotic action of the other herb. Cayenne boosts the power of Garlic so much it's akin to taking liquid penicillin.

Together, Garlic and Cayenne lower blood pressure safely and rapidly.

Cayenne is used in formulas for pain relief, infection, respiratory ailments, female problems, thyroid balance and heart treatments. Cayenne is an ingredient in laxatives, diuretics and ulcer medication. Added to Ginger, Cayenne helps clean out the bronchial tubes. Regardless of what ailment the herbal formula is designed to treat, the addition of Cayenne speeds the circulation thereby aiding the absorption and effectiveness of the formula.

Internally, Cayenne has many benefits as a catalyst and a stimulant. This powerful stimulant can also be used as a relaxant to soothe gas, diarrhea, asthma and toothaches.

Proven effective in healing gastric ulcers, Cayenne has been recommended as a gargle for a sore throat and as a hangover cure. In the West Indies, natives who are feeling feverish sip a concoction of hot water, Cayenne pods, sugar and sour orange juice. West Indians favor a local dish called "Mandram" to aid digestion. The culinary delight combines cayenne, sliced cucumbers, shallots, onions, lemon juice and Madeira wine.

Externally, the aromatic herb makes a very effective pain killer or anesthetic. Cayenne has been used in poultices for centuries as an irritant or counter-irritant. Exposure to the pungent herb can cause pain but prolonged exposure deadens the nerves to pain.

Folk medicine prescribes Cayenne powder, plaster, poultice, tincture and ointment for a variety of aches and pains including arthritis, rheumatism and bursitis. One remedy for arthritis entails rubbing Cayenne tincture on the inflamed joint, wrapping it tightly in red flannel and letting it rest the night.

Cayenne has also been touted as one of the most powerful cures for hemorrhoids. Application of Cayenne ointment brings relief from hemorrhoids but it is also recommended that the patient be warned of the pungent herb's potency.

The *Dublin Medical Press* recommended in 1850 that a drop or two of Cayenne pepper extract be applied to remedy a toothache. One hundred years later, in the 1950's, Hungarian scientists injected capsaicin, or Cayenne extract, under the skin and found that it desensitized that area of the skin to pain. Mexican folklore also refers to the use of Cayenne as a pain killer and it has been applied dry on wounds.

The active analgesic (pain killer) in Cayenne is capsaicin. Capsaicin stimulates and then inhibits the transmission of pain from the skin and membranes.

Cayenne applied to wounds acts as both an analgesic and an antibiotic. Scientific literature in Bulgaria first reported on the antibacterial benefits of Cayenne in 1927.

A Hungarian experiment showed that Cayenne inhibits the growth of several strains of bacteria and the more of the herb the investigators used the stronger the effect. In the 1960's, Hungarian scientists discovered a saponin they named capsicidin in Cayenne to which they traced the antibiotic properties of the herb.

Application of Cayenne to wounds can kill bacteria, anesthetize the pain and, according to folklore, expel foreign objects. Mixing a little Cayenne with plantain results in a poultice that has the power to eject foreign objects embedded in the skin, according to herb legend.

Both herbal lore and scientific data affirms the power of the herb that bites back. It is the case with Cayenne more than any other herb that the whole is greater than the sum of its parts.

In all studies of the medicinal benefits of the bright red pepper, Cayenne was found to be more effective than its derivative capsaicin. Tests showed that capsaicin had negative side effects that Cayenne did not. For example, at higher levels, capsaicin damaged the cells in the gastro-intestinal system, preventing the absorption of nutrients from food. Cayenne, on the other hand, increased the body's ability to absorb and process nutrients in food.

Using only single constituents isolated from an herb ignores the beneficial principles and mitigating ingredients imbodied in the whole herb. Since the whole herb Cayenne does not seem to have the harmful side effects of capsaicin, perhaps there is an ingredient in the whole herb that counteracts that negative reaction.

Studies show that Cayenne is most beneficial for treating a variety of ailments and maintaining overall cardiovascular health if it is taken daily as a whole herb not an extract. With the advent of the gelatin capsule, people who could not tolerate the bite of the red pepper can take it with ease.

It is important to remember that a little Cayenne goes a long way. Nature made the red pepper hot for a reason so if you can't swallow too much outside the capsule, don't try to swallow too much inside the capsule.

People who don't usually eat hot spicy food should build a tolerance slowly. Remember too, that Cayenne works best in concert with a healthy diet that is low in fat and high in protein and carbohydrates.

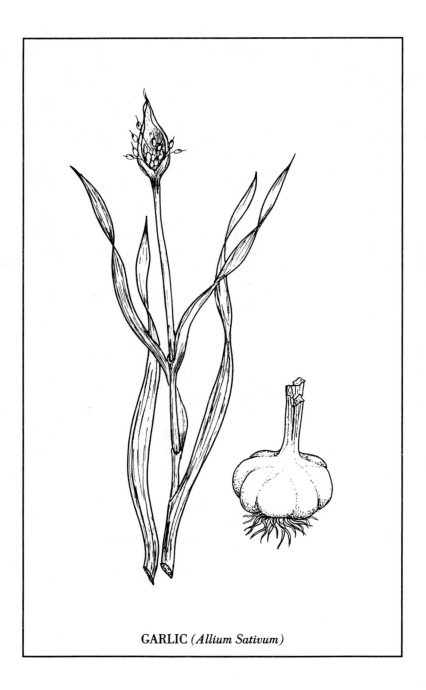

GARLIC *(Allium Sativum)*

12

GARLIC

Garlic *(latin name: Allium sativum; family: Liliaceae)* is the ultimate medicinal food. Used longer for more purposes in more places than any other plant, Garlic is touted for both its culinary and curative properties.

Unlike many herbs, the benefit of Garlic in the diet has been espoused by medical practitioners, scientists and nutritionists. Since the beginning of recorded history this kitchen medicine has been praised for its benefits to the immune, digestive, respiratory, urinary and circulatory systems.

Not a wild herb, the earliest records show Garlic was cultivated in the Middle East over 5,000 years ago. It was used for food and medicine during the reign of the Egyptian pharaohs and the earliest Chinese dynasties.

Garlic cloves were discovered in the tomb of Egyptian king Tutankhamen and were fed to the workers building the pyramids. An Egyptian medical papyrus written around 1500 B.C. listed 22 Garlic-based prescriptions for such ailments as headaches, throat problems, weakness and fatigue. The benefits of Garlic were heralded in the Bible and the Talmud.

In 460 B.C., Hippocrates, the father of medicine, was using Garlic to treat infections, intestinal disorders, wounds, chest pains and toothaches, as well as leprosy and epilepsy. Dioscorides, a physician in the Roman army during the first century A.D., prescribed Garlic to eliminate worms, soothe coughing spasms, clear arteries, heal lesions, ease premenstrual discomfort and treat scurvy.

In the first century A.D., Pliny, a Roman naturalist, listed 61 diseases that respond to Garlic. Pliny wrote of the healing power of the plant, recommending it for poisonous bites, parasites and asthma.

In China, Garlic has been used in folk medicine since around 510 A.D. to control dysentery, intestinal parasites and stomach ailments. Physicians in India during the first century consulted the Charaka-Samhita and found Garlic and Onion were recommended to ward off heart disease and rheumatism.

Traditionally, Garlic has been used in the treatment of colds, bronchitis, asthma, pneumonia, typhoid, tuberculosis, earache, sore throat, headache, stomach ache, cramps, diarrhea, dysentery, cholera worms, ulcers, high blood pressure, low blood pressure, hypertension, snakebite, gout, skin diseases and rheumatism.

Modern medicine and science has since validated what folk doctors and kitchen practitioners have known for centuries. Garlic was first recognized for its antibacterial properties in a study by Louis Pasteur in 1858. Since that time, the antibacterial action of Garlic has proven effective against forms of Staph, Strep, Brucella, Bacillus, Vibrio, Klebsiella, Proteus, Escherichia, Salmonella, Hafnia, Aeromonas, Citrobacter and Providencia.

Garlic is so effective as an antibiotic, one milligram of allicin (its major component) is about equal to 15 standard units of penicillin. Garlic works on both internal and external infections. At last count, Garlic was able to exterminate 72 separate infectious agents. Garlic is not only antibacterial but also antifungal, antiviral and antiparasitic.

By the end of the 19th century, doctors in America and Europe using Garlic to treat tuberculosis were remarking on the number of patients cured of the illness. During World War I, Garlic was used to fight typhus and dysentery and to disinfect battle wounds. Dr. Albert Schweitzer also had much success using it to treat typhus, cholera and typhoid.

In Russia, Garlic was so popular it was nicknamed "Russian Penicillin." Hospitals and clinics there use Garlic almost exclusively as an inhalant. Polish children suffering from dyspepsia, pneumonia, sepsis, nephrosis and gastroenterocolitis are treated using a Garlic preparation.

The healing properties of Garlic have been the subject of numerous studies by physicians, chemists, scientists, herbalists and nutritionists around the world. Over 1,000 papers on Garlic have been published in the last 20 years alone.

Recently, one of the most dramatic studies involved the treatment of eleven patients in China afflicted with cryptococcal meningitis which is almost always fatal. Over a period of several weeks, the patients were given Garlic extract orally and by injection. All of the patients recovered from the disease.

Garlic has proven effective in killing the organisms responsible for fungal infections like cryptococcal meningitis but in this case, the physicians maintained that part of the startling recovery was due to Garlic's ability to boost the body's natural immune system.

Numerous studies underscored the value of Garlic as a powerful antibiotic and antifungal agent, but the plant's antiviral properties are only beginning to be explored. Two independent studies, one in Japan and one in Romania, showed Garlic offers protection against influenza viruses.

Garlic can target infections just about anywhere in the body because its potent oils are readily absorbed and transported throughout the body. It is absorbed so easily that Garlic oil or juice applied to the soles of the feet will pass through the body to the lungs so fast that it can be detected on the breath within seconds of exposure.

Garlic has the ability to diffuse completely through the all the body's barriers except the brain. Since it's so versatile, Garlic is very effective against problems in the urinary system, digestive system and the cirulatory system.

In the urinary system, Garlic's volatile oils stimulate the cleansing and purging action of the kidneys. Garlic aids digestion by inciting the production of bile. Respiratory ailments such as asthma respond to Garlic because it acts as both a decongestant and an expectorant, keeping mucus moving normally through the lungs. In Poland, doctors use Garlic to cure children afflicted with acute and chronic asthma and bronchitis.

In the circulatory system, Garlic lowers cholesterol, low density lipoproteins, blood lipids and blood pressure and raises high density lipoproteins.

Research at universities and hospitals throughout the world has irrefutably established that Garlic can lower blood serum cholesterol. In these studies, patients on a high fat diet that included Garlic had consistently lower cholesterol than patients on the same diet without the Garlic. In a 1973 experiment the serum cholesterol level of healthy volunteers fell just three hours after they ate a high fat diet with Garlic added.

In one experiment, the participants were all vegetarians. Carefully matched in age, sex and social class; the vegetarians were divided into two groups, based on whether or not they ate Garlic and Onion regularly.

Since meat was not part of either diet, there was little difference between the cholesterol levels of one group and another. However, there was a marked difference in other factors that contribute to the development of atherosclerosis (hardening of the arteries accompanied by the deposit of fat in the inner arterial walls). Those vegetarians who ate Garlic and Onion had much lower levels of beta lipoproteins, phospholipids, serum-triglycerides and plasma fibrinogen than their counterparts.

It has been theorized that allicin, the active ingredient in Garlic, blocks the body's ability to synthesize and retain cholesterol. How ever it accomplishes the feat, it is clear that Garlic restricts the rise of cholesterol and lipid in the blood and may increase the fibrinolytic activity of plasma.

Dietary Garlic has certain properties that also contribute to lower blood pressure. Garlic expands vessel walls, increasing blood flow, and helps prevent blockage by inhibiting the tendency of the blood cells to stick together and form clots.

Although the healing properties of Garlic have been established scientifically for a myriad of ailments, the plant continues to show promise for new applications. The startling results of a study conducted in 1989 show Garlic may be effective in the treatment of AIDS.

Ten AIDS patients were given Garlic extract for ten weeks while the activity of the natural killer cells and the helper/suppressor ratios in their immune systems were measured. Prior to the start of the study, patients had abnormal readings in both areas.

After six weeks, six of seven patients had normal killer cell activity and four of seven patients had an improved killer/suppressor ratio. In addition, there was an improvement seen in patients suffering from AIDS-related conditions including diarrhea, candidiasis, genital herpes and pansinusitis accompanied by fever. The test group was considered small but the results were by no means insignificant.

Garlic's effect on the immune system's killer cells was the subject of a 1973 experiment performed at the Akbar Clinic and Research Center in Panama City, Florida. A team of researchers led by Dr. Tarig Abdullah took part in a study of Garlic's ability to increase the power of the immune system to ward off infectious diseases and cancer.

In the experiment, nine people including Dr. Abdullah and the other researchers ate large doses of raw Garlic every day while nine others took Kyolic, a Japanese Garlic extract; and the remaining nine did not eat Garlic at all. Blood samples were taken and the natural killer cells in the blood were mixed with cancer cells. The killer cells taken from the participants who ate raw Garlic or took Kyolic destroyed between 140 and 160 percent more cancer cells than the killer cells from the subjects who did not eat any Garlic.

A comparison of two counties in the Shandong province of China gives credence to the theory that people who make Garlic a regular part of their diet are more likely to escape the ravages of cancer.

The residents of Gangshan County are fond of Garlic and eat about seven cloves a day. Gangshan county has a gastric cancer death rate of 3.45 per 100,000 population. Meanwhile, in nearby Quixia County residents eschew Garlic and rarely indulge in the pungent plant. Quixia County residents die of gastric cancer at a rate of 40 per 100,000. Simply put, non-Garlic eaters are 12 times more likely to die of gastric cancer than their neighbors.

Investigators at the M.D. Anderson Hospital in Houston tested sulfur compounds from Garlic and discovered that the substances kept mice from developing colon cancer by thwarting the conversion of chemicals into harmful carcinogens. Sulfur compounds from Garlic are high on the National Cancer Institute's list of viable natural "chemopreventives."

In addition to fighting illness, Garlic improves overall health because of the plant's enormous nutritional value. Garlic contains high levels of protein, vitamin A, vitamin C, thaimine, and trace minerals such as iron, zinc, copper, calcium, tin, potassium, selenium, aluminum, sulfur and germanium.

Garlic, a cure for a multitude of illness, can also be taken several ways. Garlic should never be boiled because that destroys the active components that make the plant so beneficial. In fact, allicin, the component that embodies the healing power of Garlic, is not formed until the Garlic clove or bulb is cut. When the bulb is cut, the enzyme alliinase mixes with alliin to form allicin. Allicin is responsible for Garlic's curative powers and its pungent odor. Uncut Garlic bulbs do not smell.

In Italy where eating Garlic is a culinary tradition, it is customary to finish the meal with a sprig of Parsley which is rich in chlorophyll and absorbs the odor of Garlic. Garlic can be eaten as a seasoning; swallowed as a tea, juice, syrup, tincture or capsule; applied in a poultice; rubbed on the body as an oil or inhaled as a vapor.

Garlic is best used fresh. Raw Garlic destroys bacteria, boosts the immune system and may help prevent cancer. Cooked Garlic lowers cholesterol, thins the blood, acts a decongestant and expectorant. The rule of thumb is: "eat it both ways, eat it either way, but by all means eat it."

Garlic is readily absorbed and transported by the body so using the plant in any form is beneficial. However, some suggested forms of application have been put forth during its centuries of use as a kitchen medicine. For example, a clove of crushed Garlic in a glass of warm milk is recommended for spasms, cramps and seizures.

One teaspoon of Garlic syrup three times a day before meals is the traditional treatment for coughs, colds, sore throats, congestion, heart weakness, high or low blood pressure and nervous disorders.

To make Garlic syrup, put a pound of peeled minced Garlic in a two quart jar and fill it almost to the top with equal parts of apple cider vinegar and distilled water. Cover, put the jar in a warm place and let stand four days, shaking occasionally. Add one cup of glycerine and let the mixture stand for another day. Strain and filter the concoction through a cloth. Add a cup of honey, stir well and store the syrup in a cool place.

A teaspoon of Garlic oil every hour is suggested for colds, flus and fevers. The oil should be dropped into the ear to treat an earache and rubbed directly on sprains and minor skin disorders.

To make oil of Garlic, put eight ounces of peeled minced Garlic into a jar with enough olive oil to cover it. Cover the jar, put it in a warm place and let it stand shaking it occasionally. Strain the oil through a natural cotton cloth and store in a cool place. Shake Garlic oil well before using so it is thoroughly mixed.

A Garlic douche can be made for the treatment of yeast infections by blending a clove of Garlic or two Garlic capsules and one pint of water. Strain the mixture and add one or more pints of water.

GINGER *(Zingiber Officinale)*

13
GINGER

G inger *(latin name: Zingiber officinale; family: Zingi-beraceae),* has been used in Chinese medicine for over 2,000 years as a remedy for digestive disorders, nausea, fever, coughing, diarrhea, rheumatism and lumbago. Studies of Ginger root have shown the plant prevents motion sickness, thins blood, lowers cholesterol, forestalls the flu and prevents cancer in animals.

Native to coastal India, Ginger is cultivated in Jamaica, China, Africa, India and the West Indies. In Britain, only Jamaican Ginger is considered of pharmacopoeial quality. Used for centuries to detoxify meat, today Ginger is most commonly used by the food industry to flavor ginger snaps, ginger bread, ginger ale, ginger beer and assorted candies and baked goods.

Practitioners of folk medicine brewed Ginger tea to treat indigestion, stomach ache, nausea, whooping cough, malaria and fever. Externally, Ginger oil cools inflammations, eases earaches and treats dandruff. Hong Kong boat-dwellers chew it for motion sickness.

Studies have since confirmed Ginger root's effectiveness in the treatment of stomachic, digestive and circulatory disorders. Much of the research done on the plant's anti-nausea properties concentrated on treatment of motion sickness because those experiments were easiest to control.

In one test, people prone to motion sickness were placed in a spinning tilted chair designed to make the stomach churn. Twenty minutes before the test began, each member of the three groups was given a capsule. One group's capsules contained powdered Ginger root, another group's capsule contained Dramamine and the last contained only a placebo.

The patients who took Dramamine or the placebo lasted less than six minutes in the chair before they grew nauseated or vomited. Meanwhile, half of the patients who took the equivalent of half a teaspoon of powdered Ginger root completed their ride in the chair without suffering any ill effects.

Clearly, Ginger is more effective in the treatment of motion sickness than Dramamine, the most common over-the-counter drug. Unlike Dramamine, which contains the drug dimenhydrinate, Ginger does not have the side effect of drowsiness because it works on the stomach not the brain.

Gentler motion sickness studies performed by Daniel Mowrey, director of the Mountain West Institute of Herbal Science, found that Ginger worked for 90 percent of the subjects who took two to four capsules prior to travel and two more capsules every hour or at the earliest sign of an upset stomach. Ginger root proved to be an effective motion sickness antidote for travel by car, boat, train or plane.

Mowrey, who has a doctorate in psychology and psycho-pharmacology, tested Ginger root on other types of nausea and found the plant to be effective in dispelling morning sickness, dizziness, vertigo and stomach flu.

Ginger has been clinically proven to decrease the nausea, vomiting and diarrhea associated with the common three-day and 24 hour flu viruses. Taken early enough, Ginger can help thwart the flu entirely, according to Mowrey.

Mowrey recommends that 6-10 capsules be taken at the first sign of nausea or if one is caring for persons already afflicted with the virus. Timing is everything. Caught early enough, the nausea will gradually dissipate. Patients should continue to take 2-4 capsules every half hour until the nausea passes. If it is too late to avoid the onset of the virus, the capsules will not stay down. Consequently, Mowrey advises early treatment.

Ginger tea with honey and lemon is the folk medicine prescription for indigestion, cramps, nausea, colds and flu.

The tea is made by grating one ounce of fresh or dried Ginger root into a pint of water and simmering for 10 minutes.

To make a fomentation for treating external aches, pains and inflammations, simmer five ounces of grated Ginger in two quarts of water for 10 minutes. Apply the fomentation to the affected area with a cloth and re-apply to keep it warm. Reddening skin indicates increased circulation.

A massage oil for muscle pain or dandruff can be made by combining the juice of fresh grated Ginger with equal parts of sesame or olive oil. To treat an earache, put a few drops of the oil on a piece of cotton and insert into the ear.

Volatile oils, oleo resins and protein-digesting enzymes in Ginger stimulate production of digestive fluids making digestion more efficient and neutralizing acids and toxins in the digestive tract. These properties give Ginger its power to combat motion sickness, flu symptoms, stomach ailments and indigestion.

The volatile oils in Ginger also stimulate the circulatory and respiratory systems, lower cholesterol, deter blood clots and purify the blood. Ginger boosts the metabolism by increasing the function of the circulatory and respiratory system aiding the body's recovery from the negative effects of stress and fatigue.

A love of marmalade led Dr. Charles Dorso of Cornell University Medical College to the conclusion that Ginger helps prevent the formation of blood clots. Dorso was conducting an experiment using his own platelet blood cells as a "normal control" when he noticed his blood failed to coagulate in the normal way. He remembered that the night before his tests, he had indulged excessively in a tasty marmalade called Ginger and Grapefruit made by Crabtree and Evelyn of London. The major ingredient, Ginger makes up 15 percent of the marvelous marmalade.

To test his theory, the doctor mixed a little ground Ginger in test tubes with samples of his colleagues' blood. The platelets did not stick together even after he added a large amount of a substance known to stimulate blood clotting. According to Cornell researchers, it is Gingerol in the Ginger that acts as the anti-coagulent or blood thinner. Apparently, Ginger forestalls the synthesis by the blood cells of thromboxane, a substance that signals blood cells to stick together causing clotting.

In Japan, scientists contend that both fresh and processed Ginger relieves pain, lowers blood pressure and stimulates the heart. Ginger can actually block cell mutations that can lead to cancer, according to studies by Japanese scientists.

Research has shown Ginger root has the same effects whether fresh or dried. The plant can be taken confidently in large quantities because the amount that must be taken for a lethal dose is so incredibly high that the herb has been accepted as completely safe by the FDA. Ginger also enjoys a longer shelf life than most aromatic herbs because of its protective outer bark.

"Your food shall be your medicine and your medicine shall be your food."

Hippocrates

GOTU KOLA *(Centella Asiatica)*

14

GOTU KOLA

Gotu Kola *(latin name: Centella asiatica; family: Umbelli-fereae),* a common medicinal plant found in India, Pakistan, Malaysia and parts of Eastern Europe, is used to treat diseases of the skin, blood and nervous system.

A cornerstone of ayurvedic (East Indian) medicine, Gotu Kola has a long history of use for ailments of the brain and nervous system including epilepsy, schizophrenia, memory loss, depression and nervous breakdown. In addition to restoring proper function of the mind and nervous system, Gotu Kola is considered a brain food with the power to rejuvenate.

The Gotu Kola plant has long been prized in India and China for its ability to increase longevity, build mental stamina, improve the memory and retard the aging process. "A leaf or two a day will keep old age away," according to an ancient Indian proverb. Modern scientists have studied the healing and rejuvenative properties of Gotu Kola, stimulating Western interest in the plant.

Using gerbils in an activity cage, Daniel Mowry, director of the Mountain West Institute of Herbal Science, experimented with the long term effects of Gotu Kola on fatigue. Mowry, who has a doctorate in psychology and psychopharmacology, attributed the animal's increasing activity to the herb. Gotu Kola is not related to the Kola nut and does not contain the stimulant caffeine.

Studies have shown Gotu Kola to be highly effective in the treatment of fever and inflammations. In Asia and Europe it is used to cool and purify the blood by neutralizing the blood acids. Gotu Kola has been used around the world for centuries to treat leprosy, syphilis, tuberculosis, psoriasis, cervicitis, vaginitis and blisters. East Indian medicine also relies on the herb to remedy dysentery, ulcers, cholera, headaches and stomach aches. A look at the medicinal properties of Gotu Kola provides insight into the curative powers of the plant. Gotu Kola contains triterpene saponins, asiaticoside, brahmoside and brahminoside. Saponins aid the the function of the immune system by partially breaking down the walls of diseased cells, making the microbes easier to kill. Asiaticoside speeds the healing of wounds by stimulating cell division.

In addition to the four major constituents, volatile oils in the herb have a diuretic and blood purifying property and help lower serum cholesterol levels because they contain Beta-sitoerol. Flavonoids in the herb help control spasms in smooth muscles.

Gotu Kola has been found to display a broad spectrum of antibiotic activity. It can be used as an antibacterial, antifungal, antiameobic, insecticidal and anti-inflammatory agent.

The top of the Gotu Kola plant contains the medicinal qualities. The dried powdered leaves can be brewed into tea or taken in capsule form. Make the tea using 1 ounce of the herb for each pint of water. The usual dosage is 3 ounces of tea 3 times a day or 5 to 10 capsules three times a day.

Gotu Kola oil can be applied externally over the entire body including the scalp to treat nervous disorders. To make the oil, cover 1 part powdered leaves with 3 parts sesame oil, let stand covered 1 to 14 days and then filter.

"Yesterday's quackery may be today's scientific breakthrough."

HAWTHORN *(Crataegus Oxycantha)*

15

HAWTHORN

Hawthorn *(latin name: Crataegus oxycantha; family: rosaceae)* is a spiny bush native to the Mediterranean region including Northern Africa, Central Asia and all of Europe. Once sought only as a food, the brilliant red Hawthorn berries are very effective in the treatment of cardiac, circulatory and digestive ailments.

Hawthorn regulates high and low blood pressure, arrhythmic heartbeat and irregular pulse. Hawthorn prevents hardening of the arteries, treats arteriosclerosis and cools inflammation of the heart muscle. Used regularly, Hawthorn strengthens the heart muscle and the nerves to the heart.

Native Americans also use Hawthorn to treat rheumatism and bladder problems. Cooked down and concentrated berries soothe sore throats and alleviate acid conditions of the blood, according to folklore. In Italy, Hawthorn is lauded as a gentle sedative to calm the nerves and ease insomnia. Since the Tang Dynasty (618-907 A.D.) the fruits have been employed in China to improve the function of the digestive system.

In medieval England, Hawthorn was a plant surrounded by legend. In the fall, children ate the berries, called pixie pears and cuckoo's beads, which were considered quite nutritious. In the spring, its lovely white blossoms earned Hawthorn the folk names of may blossom, moon flower and white thorn. Hawthorn branches made up the maypole the children danced around during the May festival. This tradition lasted into the 1800s.

Romantic hymns were sung throughout Europe about the

legendary plant. Poets praised Hawthorn as a symbol of spring's hopefulness and love's promise. Chaucer wrote;

> *"Marke the faire blooming of the Hawthorne tree*
> *Who finely clothed in robe of white,*
> *Fills full the wanton eye with May's delight."*

It was not until the 1800's that Hawthorn was directed at aiding, rather than wooing, the heart. In Ireland, a Dr. Green had gained renown for his astounding success in the treatment of heart disease. The well-known physician kept the remedy a secret until his death in 1894. After he died, his daughter revealed his famous cure to be a tincture made from ripe red Hawthorn berries.

After Green's death, Hawthorn became widely used as a treatment for heart and cardiovascular ailments. Homeopathic and allopathic doctors in Europe experienced consistent clinical success with Hawthorn in the late 19th and early 20th centuries.

Controlled medical studies in Europe showed that Hawthorn lowered blood pressure and reduced the strain on the heart by dilating the blood vessels away from the heart, strengthened the heart muscle by increasing the metabolism of enzymes in the heart muscle, boosted the utilization of oxygen by the heart and slightly dilated the coronary vessels. Almost all the heart patients given Hawthorn showed improvement. Hawthorn normalized and enhanced the function of the heart and circulatory system without side effects.

The benefits of Hawthorn came to the attention of the American medical establishment by the end of the 1800s. Doctors lauded the plant's effectiveness and lack of side effects. Hawthorn, they said, was more effective than digitalis and strophanthin for handling chronic cardiac illness.

Studies indicate that up to 30 percent of patients taking digitalis experience symptoms of poisoning. In over a hundred years of clinical use, even when tested in extremely high levels, Hawthorn has shown no toxicity. Adding Hawthorn to digitalis and strophanthin reduces the side effects associated with the two drugs especially in older patients.

Hawthorn is a gentle heart tonic that nurtures the entire circulatory system. Hawthorn has proven effective as a treatment for functional heart disease, arrhythmia, angina pectoris, age-related circulatory insufficiency, arteriosclerosis and regulation of the circulatory system.

To thwart the damaging effects of a heart attack Hawthorn is the 'ounce of prevention that is worth a pound of cure.' Hawthorn improves coronary circulation by dilating the coronary arteries to bring more oxygen directly to the heart muscle and reducing the chances of heart attack or angina. Increasing the ability of the heart to function smoothly, Hawthorn imparts a gentle but persistent toning action that compensates for age-related degeneration of the heart. Simply put, Hawthorn helps keep the heart healthy enough to head off a heart attack.

Used in conjuction with a healthy diet and stress management, Hawthorn is the perfect preventative prescription for persons who have a family history of heart disease. Considered a safe and effective long-term treatment for the gradual loss of heart function that comes with age, Hawthorn is not habit forming, accumulative or toxic.

For patients who have already suffered a heart attack, studies show Hawthorn speeds recovery, lowers blood pressure, strengthens the heart and forestalls any onset of coronary disease. No other herb in the plant kingdom provides the nourishing regeneration of Hawthorn both before or after a heart attack.

Although the cardiovascular benefits of Hawthorn have been recognized by doctors in the United States, the plant is still not as widely used as it is in Europe. In Germany, for example, 78 of 112 herbal preparations for heart afflictions sold in pharmacies and health food stores contain Hawthorn.

For centuries, Hawthorn has been sought for both food and medicine in Europe and Asia. In the mountains around Peking, Hawthorn fruit was collected to make a sweet and sour candied fruit treat said to stimulate the digestive system. In Russia, the fruit was used to make wine.

Nutlets from the plant have been recovered at several archeological sites throughout Europe that date from the Neolithic to Roman ages. Hawthorn seeds have been discovered in Bronze Age sites in Israel.

Hawthorn has been mentioned in the writings of ancient Greece and regarded by Christians as sacred. Christian lore holds that the spiny Hawthorn tree provided the crown of thorns that Christ wore to his crucifixion. Some of the trees still stand on the Mount of Olives outside Jerusalem.

Although Hawthorn berries are used in marmalades, jellies and as a flour additive, powdered Hawthorn should be taken with the meal or shortly after eating to avoid nausea. The recommended dosage of Hawthorn, whether in capsules, powder or tincture, is three times a day.

To make the tincture, steep four ounces of the berries in a pint of brandy for two weeks, then filter. Fifteen drops is considered one dose. For Hawthorn tea, add one or two teaspoons of berries to hot water.

16

LECITHIN

Lecithin is a natural fat that breaks down fat and cholesterol enabling the body to use what it needs and discard the rest. Lecithin cleanses the circulatory system, provides essential nutrients for proper function of the brain and nervous system, helps metabolize fat soluble vitamins A, E, D and K, breaks up gallstones, improves liver function, lowers cholesterol, alleviates arteriosclerosis and clears up skin problems.

In 1850, Maurice Gobley of France isolated the substance in egg yolks that enabled water and oil to mix and named his discovery Lecithin after the Greek word "lekithos" meaning "yolk of egg." The first uses for this natural emulsifier were commercial. Used in the production of margarine, chocolate, paint and cosmetics, it wasn't until the second half of this century that the nutritional and medicinal properties of Lecithin were explored.

Shortly after production began, it was discovered that soybeans offered a purer, more nutritious and less expensive source of Lecithin than egg yolks. Egg yolks are high in Lecithin but also contain large amounts of cholesterol. Cholesterol has been inexorably linked to heart disease and arteriosclerosis. The ratio of Lecithin to cholesterol in egg yolks is such that cholesterol comes out the winner and the patient the loser. Soybeans are also high in polyunsaturated fats which help lower the blood cholesterol level.

Lecithin can also be found in nuts, whole wheat, liver and beef hearts and in the human body. Contained in all the cells and organs of the body, Lecithin makes up 30 percent of the dry weight of the brain. In the liver, where Lecithin is produced, almost two-thirds of the liver fat contains Lecithin.

Lecithin emulsifies fat in the body just like in a chocolate bar. Lecithin breaks up fat and cholesterol into little particles and suspends them in the blood stream which is mostly water. One side of the Lecithin molecule attracts fat and the other attracts water. Bound together by Lecithin, the tiny particles of fat flow through the artery walls, into the capillaries and to the cells where they are most needed.

Without Lecithin to keep the fat and cholesterol soluble, it collects on the artery walls. This condition, the narrowing and hardening of the arteries from cholesterol build-up, is known as arteriosclerosis. Arteriosclerosis can lead to heart attack and stroke.

Lecithin not only prevents cholesterol from building up on the arterial walls but also helps remove deposits that have already formed. Normally, cholesterol dissolves only at a very high temperature, but when Lecithin is introduced cholesterol will liquify at a temperature lower than normal body heat.

Once dissolved, the scouring action of normal blood flow can wash cholesterol off the arterial walls. Held in suspension by Lecithin, the newly-liquified cholesterol can pass harmlessly through the body.

Scientists found simply adding soybeans, the best available source of Lecithin, to the diet reversed arterial heart disease, lowered genetically-high cholesterol counts and counteracted the effects of a high fat diet.

In 1972, scientists at the Center for the Study of Hyperlipidemias at the University of Milan, Italy, added soybeans to the diet of patients with genetically high cholesterol counts, many over 300. The patients ate soybeans as a source of protein instead of meat and dairy products. After the change in diet, their destructive LDL (low density lipoprotein) cholesterol level fell by 15 to 20 percent. Results were the same in both adults and children.

The soybean diet not only lowered existing cholesterol levels but overcame the cholesterol-raising potential of a high fat diet. Dr. C.R. Sirtori led an experiment whereby about 500 milligrams of cholesterol (the equivalent of a couple of eggs) was added to his patient's soybean diet. According to Sirtori, the soybeans apparently overcame the extra cholesterol and kept the blood cholesterol level down.

Once their blood cholesterol level was lowered, Sirtori's patients went back to their old diet but still ate at least six meals a week containing textured soybean protein. Tracked for two more years, their blood cholesterol levels remained low.

More time on the soybean diet led to an increase in Sirtori's patients' HDL (high density lipoprotein) cholesterol levels. HDL cholesterol is the good cholesterol that removes destructive LDL cholesterol. Low HDL cholesterol levels increase the risk of heart attack.

Sirtori discovered long-term adherence to the soybean diet not only stopped the advance of arterial heart disease, but actually reversed it. After three years on the soybean diet, one woman's blood cholesterol level fell from 332 to 206 milligrams and the blood flow to her heart improved dramatically.

Investigators David Klurfeld and David Kritchevsky performed an experiment using soybeans at Philadelphia's Wistar Institute that reversed artherosclerosis in rabbits, who were raised on meat and dairy.

Artherosclerosis, like arteriosclerosis, occurs when cholesterol deposits build up on the walls of the arteries narrowing and hardening them. The condition is called artherosclerosis when it affects the coronary arteries which carry blood to the heart.

In Klurfeld and Kritchevsky's experiment, the rabbits were given soybeans as their only protein source instead of meat. Their blood cholesterol dropped 50 percent and their rate of artherosclerosis was cut in half. Klurfeld and Kritchevsky then returned meat and dairy products to the animals' diet so that soybeans now made up just half of their protein intake. Even then, the blood cholesterol level and rate of atherosclerosis stayed down at half what it was before the introduction of soybeans. Soybeans rejuvenated the rabbits' arteries.

As a cholesterol and fat fighter, Lecithin targets not only the circulatory system, but also the liver and gallbladder. Lecithin breaks up gallstones which are composed mainly of hardened cholesterol. Gallstones are formed if the bile is unable to digest fat properly. Lecithin in the bile helps emulsify the fat and prevent gallstones from forming.

Lecithin increases fat metabolism preventing gallstones from forming, cleansing artery walls and keeping fat from collecting in the liver. If the liver does not produce a sufficient supply of Lecithin, body fats or triglycerides accumulate in the liver, resulting in sluggish liver function. Cells in the liver fill with fat and become swollen and inflamed.

Lecithin contains choline and inositol, B vitamins responsible for helping metabolize fat. Inositol also stimulates hair growth and aids in digestion. Studies indicate that inositol in Lecithin may benefit diabetics by helping to correct impaired glucose tolerance and keep insulin levels under control. Soybeans added to the diet regulate blood sugar.

Liathinose, an enzyme produced by the body, unlocks the choline in Lecithin. The choline is the catalyst that changes fat so it does not accumulate in the liver. In addition to helping maintain a healthy liver, Lecithin helps correct problems resulting from deficiencies of choline and other nutritional substances in the kidneys.

Incidentally, choline taken alone has side effects not encountered with Lecithin. Bacteria in some individuals breaks down choline. As a result, the choline is rendered ineffective and the people smell like dead fish.

In addition, a study sponsored by the Food and Drug Administration (FDA) found that taking large doses of choline can lead to nausea, vomiting, salivation, sweating and anorexia and that straight choline was only effective for a short time. Lecithin had none of these side effects and proved to be longer acting, resistant to bacterial attack and easier to tolerate.

Choline is one of the few substances able to break through

the brain blood barrier. In the brain, choline stimulates the production of acetylcholine, a neurotransmitter. Neurotransmitters are the chemical messengers that conduct information through the nervous system bridging the gap between individual neurons and muscle cells. Neurons, tiny nerve cells, control every aspect of behavior including mood, memory, thought, speech, sensation and movement. It is not clear what specific area acetylcholine targets, but the nervous system cannot function properly without a sufficient amount of it.

Acetylcholine is essential for proper brain function. Choline, produced in the liver or obtained by eating Lecithin, enhances the operation of the brain and stimulates the brain cells to produce more acetylcholine.

Fledgling research indicates that choline from Lecithin may be able to boost memory and counteract depression and dementia traced to a deficiency of acetylcholine. Startling results were achieved using choline and Lecithin to treat Tardive Dyskinesia, a disabling brain disorder caused by failure of the brain cells to release acetylcholine.

A common ailment among mental patients, Tardive Dyskinesia is triggered by the powerful drugs used to treat the symptoms of mental illness. Some estimate that as many as 40 percent of elderly long-time psychiatric patients suffer from the condition which causes involuntary muscle spasms and twitches in the mouth, upper body and arms. Speech becomes difficult and movement uncontrollable in these patients. The symptoms can become psychologically damaging and inhibit the use of the drugs prescribed to treat the original ailment.

Studies confirmed choline suppresses the involuntary movements associated with Tardive Dyskinesia. Use of choline and Lecithin, a dietary source of choline, to treat the condition is now standard procedure.

Experiments using Lecithin to treat other disorders traced to acetylcholine deficiencies such as Alzheimer's Disease are already showing promise. Alzheimer's Disease is characterized by memory loss and irrational behavior. Studies on rats have already demonstrated that Lecithin can enhance short-term memory and it also has been effective in treating certain types of mania.

In addition to boosting production of a crucial neuro-transmitter, Lecithin helps rebuild damaged nerve tissue relieving problems such as insomnia, irritability and impatience.

Multiple sclerosis, a degenerative nerve disease, has been linked to Lecithin deficiency or depletion. Autopsies revealed lower levels of Lecithin in the brain and in the myelin sheath which shields the nerves.

The severity and frequency of attacks decreased for multiple sclerosis patients who adhered to diets containing oils that stimulate Lecithin production or took Lecithin supplements. When the diet lacked nutritional sources of Lecithin, the severity of the symptoms increased.

Demographic studies have also revealed that in locations where the typical diet is high in saturated fat, the incidence of multiple sclerosis is higher than in areas where a diet high in polyunsaturated fat is favored. Lecithin contains a high amount of linoleic acid, an essential fatty acid found in certain types of polyunsaturated fat. Scientists theorize that it is the linoleic acid in Lecithin that accounts for its success in the treatment of multiple sclerosis. Researchers have stated that the essential fatty acids, such as linoleic acid, found in Lecithin are 50 times more active than those contained in other dietary sources.

Too much saturated fat in the diet has also been estab-lished as the leading cause of coronary thrombosis, a fatal heart disease. Coronary thrombosis can result when blood clots form in the blood stream. If the clots get big enough, they can block the flow of blood to the heart resulting in a heart attack. If arteriosclerois is present, the chances of the clots cutting off blood flow from the narrowed arteries increases exponentially.

Excessive blood fats increase the production of fibrinogen which causes the blood cells to get sticky and start clumping together forming blood clots. While eating saturated fats increases the chance of blood clots forming, a diet emphasizing polyunsaturated fats has the opposite effect.

Researchers believe that it is the linolenic acid in polyunsaturated fats that inhibits the production of fibrinogen and keeps clots from forming. Lecithin is rich in linolenic acid and linoleic acid, another essential fatty acid. The body cannot produce linoleic acid itself, but, when a sufficient supply is available, the body uses linoleic acid to manufacture other essential fatty acids.

Essential fatty acids are necessary for the body to perform a variety of functions. Healthy skin thrives on proper use of fatty acids. Blemishes and skin diseases are often the result of glitches in the metabolism of fat into useful fatty acids. Lecithin has been used successfully to treat eczema, seborrhoea, psoriasis and certain types of acne. By enabling the body to metabolize fat and utilize essential fatty acids, Lecithin provides both the fuel and the oil to keep the engine of the body running smoothly.

The body stores its own supply of energy in unsightly fat deposits referred to colloquially as "love handles," "spare tires" and "cottage cheese thighs." Technically a fat itself, Lecithin is a fat-fighter that targets bad fat wherever it may be.

Lecithin breaks up the fat deposits, freeing them for the body to use. Keeping fat in suspension and free-flowing, Lecithin prevents new deposits from collecting by assuring the fat is burned quickly and efficiently. Lecithin itself burns fat faster than any other nutrient. A natural diuretic, Lecithin eases water weight gain while breaking up and burning fat.

The ability of Lecithin to emulsify fat also helps the body absorb fat-soluble vitamins A and E which help keep the heart healthy.

Vitamin E strengthens and rebuilds capillaries, keeps damaged tissue soft and flexible, inhibits the formation of blood clots and increases the ability of the circulatory system to provide blood and oxygen to the heart while decreasing the heart's need for oxygen. Vitamin A helps reduce blood cholesterol levels and stimulates natural Lecithin production.

Soybeans offer the best source of dietary Lecithin. To make Lecithin supplements, soybeans are rolled into thin flakes and the oil extracted. Water is added to the raw oil which is then heated. The Lecithin in the mixture swells and can be spun off from the soybean oil using separators. The result is a Lecithin oil containing at least two-thirds phospholipids (Lecithin) to one-third soybean oil. This oil is what is contained in high-quality Lecithin supplement capsules.

The quality of the Lecithin supplement depends on the proportion of phospholipids it contains. Look for supplements with a phospholipid content of no less than 98 percent and a high proportion of phosphatidyl choline. Phosphatidyl choline approximates the kind of Lecithin present in the heart. The higher the phosphatidyl choline content, the purer the Lecithin supplement.

To make a higher quality grandular or powdered supplement, raw Lecithin oil is dehydrated. Most of the soybean oil is removed so the resulting purer mixture contains only about two percent soybean oil to 99 percent phospholipid (Lecithin) and a touch of vitamin E. A natural antioxidant, vitamin E helps keep Lecithin from going bad and getting rancid.

Caution must be taken when searching for a high quality Lecithin supplement. Label information on this supplement is more misleading than any other. Beware of imitation granules which contain only about 30 percent Lecithin.

There are a few tip-offs when trying to spot low quality Lecithin. For example, pure Lecithin contains no protein, and a label listing a calcium content of around 6% of the recommended daily allowance signals the presence of an additive like tricalcium phosphate. Also, pure Lecithin doesn't absorb moisture rapidly so if the label reads "instantly dispersable" it may contain whey or milk solids.

Pure granular Lecithin devoid of additives and preservatives is the most potent source of Lecithin.

Granular Lecithin can be sprinkled on cereal, mixed in hot drinks or eaten by the spoonful. Nutritionists recommend starting a Lecithin regimen by taking three tablespoons of

Lecithin granules once a day for 12 days. This program, designed to clear clogged arteries, is called the 12-Day Flush. After cleansing the circulatory system with 12-Day Flush, nutritionists recommend taking a tablespoon or two a day to maintain good health.

In his book titled *A Year of Health and Beauty*, Vidal Sassoon reveals Lecithin as an important ingredient in his famous vitality drink. To make the drink, add one tablespoon of Lecithin powder, two tablespoons protein powder and a bit of bran and wheat germ to two cups of skim milk, an egg and a banana. Blend the mixture for half a minute and serve. Other fruits or orange juice can be substituted for the banana and the egg is optional. Perfect for breakfast, the drink keeps well in the refrigerator.

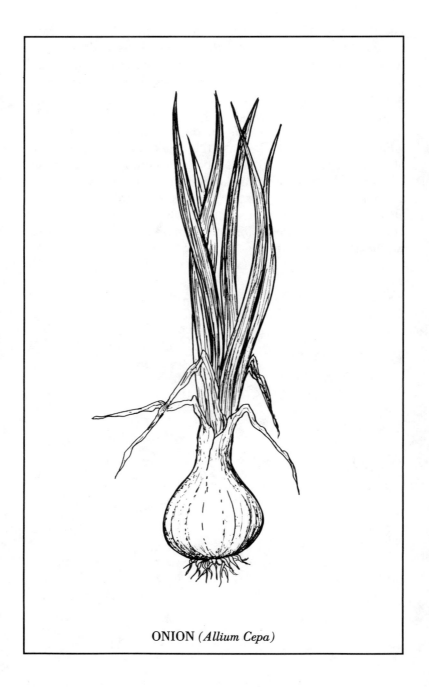

ONION *(Allium Cepa)*

17

ONION

Onion *(latin name: Allium cepa; family: Lilaceae)* has been lauded for both its medicinal benefits and its culinary contributions for over 5,000 years. Like Garlic, its herbal cousin, Onion has been looked upon as cure-all in folk medicine and prescribed for almost every scurge afflicting man or beast.

No ordinary cooking herb, Onion has been used throughout recorded history as a heart tonic, blood purifier, expectorant, antibiotic, contraceptive, diuretic, blood thinner, antiseptic, digestive aid, sedative and aphrodisiac.

One of the first plants to be cultivated, Onion has been used for centuries all over the world to treat such ailments as arthritis, arteriosclerosis, asthma, bronchitis, baldness, cholera, colds, cancer, constipation, diabetes, dandruff, dysentery, dropsy, dyspepsia, epilepsy, gangrene, hypertension, influenza, gas, jaundice, laryngitis, leprosy, lead poisoning, malaria, measles, meningitis, rheumatism, ringworm, scurvy, smallpox, tuberculosis and typhoid.

An Onion a day was the prescription Dr. Victor Gurewich, a professor of medicine at Tufts University, gave his heart patients to help boost their low HDL cholesterol levels. HDL (high density lipoprotein) cholesterol is the good type of cholesterol that removes the destructive LDL cholesterol from the blood to the liver where it can be destroyed. High HDL cholesterol levels offer protection against the damaging effects of blood cholesterol and heart attack. Low HDL levels increase the risk of heart attack.

Dr. Gurewich's patients had all suffered heart attacks and their HDL levels were well below the normal 25 percent reading. Gurewich had tried several conventional treatments without avail when a colleague from Poland suggested Onions. The fellow doctor had read folklore about the benefits of Onions including a recommendation in an ancient Egyptian papyrus.

Dr. Gurewich, director of the vascular laboratory at St. Elizabeth's Hospital in Boston and a leading cardiologist, was already familiar with some of Onion's benefits to the blood. He also knew there would be no side effects unlike commonly prescribed therapeutic drugs.

Gurewich started his patients on one medium-sized raw Onion a day either whole or in capsules. After a month of treatment the HDL levels of Gurewich's patients rose an average of 30 percent, boosting them into the normal range. With further study, Gurewich found that only half a medium raw Onion was as effective as a whole Onion.

Heat damaged Onion's ability to stimulate the production of HDL cholesterol so cooked Onions had little effect on HDL levels. The stronger and fresher the Onion, the more dramatic the increase in HDL levels.

In addition to Onion's effect on HDL cholesterol, Gurewich discovered a myriad of other cardiovascular benefits.

Cooked or raw Onions contain adenosine, a compound known to lower blood pressure by inhibiting the tendency of platelets to stick together and form clots. Besides preventing clots from forming, Onion stimulates the body's fibrinolytic system helping to dissolve clots that have already formed. This is very important because, according to the famous Framingham Heart Study of Massachusetts, men with high levels of fibrinogen (the substance that forms the clots) are good candidates for strokes and coronary artery disease.

Studies show an abundance of fibrinogen in the blood can be more dangerous than high blood pressure. Blood clots can obstruct the arteries cutting off the oxygen that sustains the heart muscle and brain cells. Onions attack fibrinogen.

Additionally, by stimulating the fibrinolytic system to kill the fibrinogen, Onions also offset the damage done by a high fat diet. High fat meals boost clot-forming fibrinogen, thicken blood and increase detrimental cholesterol levels.

Adding Onion to a high fat diet lowered blood cholesterol, thinned blood, prevented platelet clumping and inhibited blood clotting according to a 1966 study by Dr. N. N. Gupta at K.G. Medical College in Lucknow, India. Just two ounces of lightly fried Onions added to a meal packed with ninety percent fat including butter, cream and eggs, proved to be a powerful antidote to the ill effects associated with a high fat diet.

Whether boiled, raw, dried or fried, subsequent studies showed Onions partially cleaned the blood of polluting effects of a diet high in fat. In view of these findings, it seems wise to top your burger with Onion or sprinkle it in that cheese souffle.

The French added Onions to their horses' diet to help break up blood clots in the beasts' legs. Obviously, they were aware of the blood-thinning properties of Onion.

In 1923, researchers found that Onion also lowered blood sugar. Indian researchers discovered that raw Onion, boiled Onion and Onion extract lowered blood sugar in patients who had just taken glucose. In Egypt, pharmacists recently isolated a compound in Onion that lowered blood sugar in hyperglycemic rabbits more effectively than the commonly prescribed drug tolbutamide.

Onion's value as a natural antibiotic was first established in the West by Louis Pasteur. In the mid-1800s Pasteur declared both Garlic and Onion antibacterial. Onion has proven itself in battle against a long list of deadly bacteria including E. coli and Salmonella.

Doctors treating Soviet soldiers' wounds during World War II, reported rapid relief of pain and quick healing using the vapors from Onion paste. The Soviets also employed Onion as an antiseptic. Chief Investigator B. Tokin, a Soviet scientist claimed that chewing raw onion for 3-8 minutes sterilized the mouth.

George Washington lauded Onions as a cure for the common cold. If he had a cold, Washington said he ate a hot roasted Onion before bed.

Dr. Irwin Ziment agreed with Washington's estimation of Onion as a cold remedy. Dr. Ziment, a pulmonary specialist, said the pungent qualities of Onion breaks up the mucous in the lungs and help move it into the throat where it can be coughed up. As an expectorant, Onion is beneficial in the treatment of chronic bronchitis, according to Dr. Ziment.

The value of Onion in preventing cancer is beginning to be explored in earnest. Recent studies have found that concentrated sulfur compounds in Onion can turn off cell changes preceding cancer development. Propylsulfide in Onion blocked the action of enzymes needed to unleash potent cancer-causing substances according to a study by the M. D. Anderson Hospital and Tumor Institute.

In addition to promising results showing Onion's ability to prevent cancer, the plant may stop the spread of cancer that has already started to grow. Researchers at the Harvard School of Dental Medicine put Onion extract on oral cancer cells from animals and found that it inhibited the growth of the cancer cells and even destroyed some of them. Encouraged by Onion's demonstrated ability to fend off cancer, the National Cancer Institute is funding further study.

When using Onion to treat a variety of ailments from the common cold to heart disease, the rule of thumb is "more is better." Onion benefits most those who eat it most often.

Half a medium size raw Onion a day boosts the good HDL cholesterol level by up to 30 percent. Just a tablespoon of cooked Onions or about two ounces of raw ones offers a potent antidote for the blood pollution caused by a high fat meal. Raw or cooked, half a cup of Onions a day will keep your circulatory system in good shape.

With today's modern medical science,
"we need a double-blind, controlled
study published in a peer-reviewed
medical journal to prove that apples
fall from trees before we can accept the
concept of gravity."

Hans Selye,
Clinical Trial vs Clinical Judgement

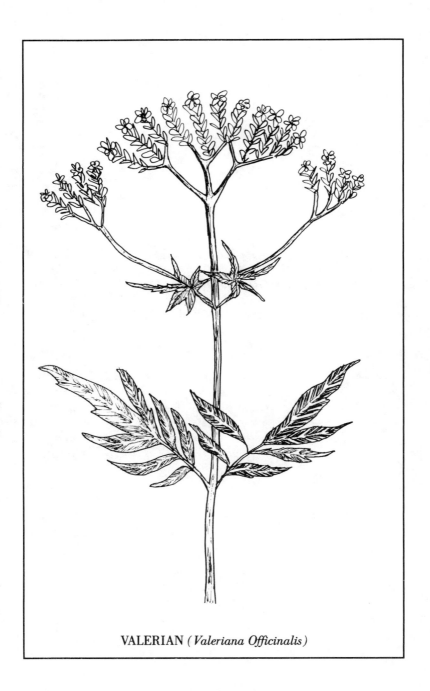

VALERIAN (*Valeriana Officinalis*)

18

VALERIAN

Valerian *(latin name: Valeriana officinalis; family: Valeri-anaceae)* has been used for over 1,000 years as a sedative, antispasmodic and diuretic. Although Valerian is native to England, Europe and North America, other varieties of the herb grow wild in China, the Far East and South America. Cultivated in Holland, Germany, Russia and Mexico, the plant grows up to 4 feet high with rough serrated dark green leaves and a crown of white, pink or lavender flowers.

The root of the Valerian plant, which emanates a putrid odor similar to that of bad cheese or mildewed clothing, has the power to soothe the nerves, quiet heart palpitations, stimulate digestion, strengthen the circulatory system, heal ulcers, relax and smooth muscles, relieve anxiety, ease hypertension and calm hyperactivity.

Dioscorides, a physician in the Roman army during the first century A.D., prescribed Valerian for headaches, digestive problems, urinary tract disorders, flatulence and nausea. Dioscorides called the herb "phu" which translates as the colloquial expression "pew," referring to the root's foul smell.

The name Valerian is said to be taken from the Latin "valene" which means "to be strong" or the Latin "valere" which means "to be in health." Incidentally, cats love the smell of Valerian which has the same intoxicating effect on them as catnip.

Despite its repulsive odor, German ladies are said to have taken Valerian in their coffee to keep them calm and worry-free. Valerian was was prescribed to treat the "vapors" in females of all ages, from pre-teen to post-menopausal. Symptoms of the "vapors" ranged from fainting and convulsions to anxiety and irrational fears, according to medical materials from the 19th century.

Peasants in medieval England considered Valerian an essential ingredient for tasty soups and stews. Today, Valerian extracts and oils are used to flavor beverages, baked goods, desserts and candies. Surprisingly, Valerian has even been used as a perfume!

Traditionally, Valerian has been used medicinally to treat nervous disorders, hypochondria, migraines, insomnia, depression, cramps, croup, colic, flatulence, whooping cough, typhoid, fever, epilepsy, vertigo, convulsions, diabetes, cholera, sores, heart palpitations, stomach ulcers, vaginal yeast infections, premenstral syndrome, bed-wetting and sleep disorders. In Indochina, Valerian is used to cool inflammation. Hyperactive children in Argentina are given Valerian tea to drink.

The use of Valerian as a sedative pre-dates the Christian calendar and has been written about in almost every pharmacological source in the world. In the second century A.D., Greek physician Galen was using Valerian to treat epilepsy with much success. Valerian was particularly successful against seizures triggered by strong emotions like fear and anger.

Fabio Colonna, a wealthy Italian nobleman in the 1500's, stumbled upon the writings of Galen while searching for a cure for his epilepsy. Legend has it that Colonna took Valerian in half-teaspoon doses and was restored to full health. Inspired, Colonna went on to become a widely read botanical author. His personal account of how Valerian ended his life-long struggle with epilepsy generated an interest in Valerian that lasted five centuries.

Two hundred years after Fabio Colonna found his cure, renowned 18th century physician William Cullen reported that Valerian was only effective in some cases of epilepsy but that it was most valuable as an antispasmodic and sleep aid. By the late 19th century, Valerian was commonly prescibed to treat nervous disorders and promote sleep. Valerian was listed as an official and accepted drug in the *United States Pharmacopeia* from 1820-1942 and in the *National Formulary* from 1888-1950.

Hundreds of experiments have been conducted on Valerian primarily in Germany and Russia. These studies have substanciated the herb's effectiveness in the treatment of nervous, circulatory, digestive and sleep disorders. Valerian root targets the higher brain centers, suppressing and regulating the autonomic nervous system. Consequently, Valerian is very effective in dispelling pyschosomatic diseases which result from a glitch in the regulation of the autonomic nervous system. Valerian pacifies the fears of hypochondriacs, soothes the nervous and calms the hysterical.

For over 10 years, Valerian has been employed in Germany to treat children with behavioral disorders such as hyperactivity.

In one study, 120 children afflicted with various psychosomatic ailments and behavioral disorders including anxiety, hyperactivity and learning disabilities were given Valmane for several weeks. At the end of that time, over three-fourths of the children had either made remarkable progess or recovered completely. Valmane is a highly tested German drug containing pure Valerian root.

The preparation enhanced the children's coordination while relieving their anxiety and calming their fears. Even at high doses, Valerian and Valmane have no side effects unlike many drugs commonly used to treat anxiety and hyperactivity.

Adults suffering from anxiety and emotional disturbances were the subject of an Italian study. The 40 patients were divided equally into two groups. One group was given two 50 mg. Valerian tablets three times a day for 21 days. The other group was given a placebo. Valerian was found to be statistically superior in the treatment of emotional disturbances without side effects.   Unlike barbituates taken to induce sleep or quiet anxiety, Valerian acts as an effective sedative without lingering drowsiness. Valerian does not interact with alcohol so there is no resulting depression or dangerous synergism associated with mixing a tranquilizer like Valium with alcohol.

Unlike Valerian, taking synthetic sedatives like Valium can lead to addiction and loss of locomotor coordination. One clinical herbalist recommends using Valerian to safely wean patients addicted to synthetic sedatives.

During the 1980's, P.D. Leatherwood, F. Chauffard and several of their colleagues at the Nestle Corporation in Switzerland published the results of several studies of the effects of Valerian on sleep patterns.

In one of the studies, sleep quality was measured by the subjects themselves but reinforced with EEG readings. After taking Valerian, all 128 volunteers reported improvement in sleep latency, which is the time it takes to fall asleep; and sleep quality or soundness of sleep. Restless sleepers and insomniacs showed the most improvement. Dream recall was not affected.

All the subjects reported falling asleep faster, sleeping better and waking refreshed. Valerian did not produce the "hang-over" effect that is a common complaint of patients using synthetic sleep aids.

Hypertensive men were the subject of another Leatherwood study using Valerian. The men drank a glass of water containing Valerian root extract and experienced a tranquilizing effect. EEG (electroencepholograph) readings revealed the herb had an elective neurotropic action on the higher brain centers.

In addition to easing stress and reducing hypertension, studies show that Valerian slows the heart rate while increasing the power of each beat, making the action of the heart more efficient and less strained. Since Valerian also regulates the heart beat, it is very effective in the treatment of heart palpitations. In Guatemala, Valerian is a key ingredient in an herb preparation used to lower blood pressure.

In addition to its benefits for the circulatory system, studies show Valerian eases gastrointestinal ailments and aids digestion. The herb stimulates secretions in the stomach and the intestines, helping heal and prevent ulcers.

Whether taken in a tincture, tea or capsule, Valerian has proven to be one of the safest and most effective sedatives available. In the United States, Valerian has been approved as a GRAS (generally recognized as safe) ingredient and is commonly used in a variety of food and beverage products ranging from alcoholic drinks to frozen desserts. Until about a decade ago, tincture of Valerian could be found on the shelves of pharmacies across the United States, but now it is an anomaly.

In Germany, Valerian has been approved for use in sedatives and sleep aids for treatment of nervous disorders and difficulty sleeping. Valerian is used in several patent medicines in Europe.

Although Valerian can be taken in a variety of ways including elixir, extract, infusion, powder, solid or tincture, the herb should never be boiled since much of its theurapeutic value is in the essential oils which would dissipate. The herb can be preserved in glycerin without any loss of potency.

Fresh or recently dried Valerian root contains the most beneficial properties. Older long-dried roots are far less potent and have a stronger smell and sharper taste than fresh. Like Garlic, fresh Valerian root has little aroma until it is scratched, cut or crushed. As Valerian dries, an enzymatic change produces an odorous compound. As a general rule, the more time Valerian root has to age, the weaker and fouler smelling it becomes.

Studies showed that Valerian tincture was only effective in a large enough dose. One full teaspoon of tincture relieved smooth muscle spasms, induced sleep and acted as a sedative.

Folk medicine recommends Valerian tea for insomnia. This recipe for a good night's sleep calls for half a teaspoon of Valerian root mixed with hot water and little sugar or honey. Taken hot, the tea also encourages menstruation and eases cramps, according to ancient practitioners. For treatment of pimples and sores, one should drink Valerian tea while applying the herb externally to the affected area.

Adding Valerian to other herb formulas enhances their tonic, antispasmodic and nervine properties. For example, a combination of hot Valerian and Cayenne pepper has been used to treat hysteria, convulsions and colic. A folk recipe for antispasmodic powder calls for one ounce each of Valerian, Scullcap and Skunk Cabbage and one-quarter ounce each of Lobelia, Cinnamon and Cayenne.

PART III

THE HEART

by Colin Quinn

*In the U.S., we do bypass surgery
twice as often as Canada and Australia
and more than four times as often
as Western Europe.*

"If the doctor of today does not become the dietician of tomorrow, the dietician of today will become the doctor of tomorrow."

Dr. Alexis Carrel
Rockefeller Institute of Medical Research

19

TECHNIQUES OF DIAGNOSIS

In order to receive proper and beneficial treatment the diagnosis must be correct. The following are the most popular techniques used by doctors to determine the condition of a person's heart muscles and arteries.

Electrocardiogram (EKG)

The muscles of the heart (like all muscles) are activated by minute electronic pulses. By monitoring these pulses, as each muscle of the heart contracts and then relaxes, doctors can determine if the heart is functioning abnormally.

The procedure is non-invasive (no opening of the skin), painless and totally without risk. A set of sensors is placed on certain strategic parts of the chest, and a readout of the heart's beating cycle is shown on a monitor or printed out on a strip of paper.

Theoretically, if the person's heart is healthy, the readout should conform, for the most part, to the doctor's model heart profile. If it doesn't, the doctor will use the parts of the patient's profile that are different to see which muscles are damaged. Unfortunately, it is not as easy as that. Because people's heart rhythms are all slightly different, it is not easy to define what is "normal" or "abnormal."

Often, it is necessary to have more than one EKG, or to

take a Stress EKG, because the results of the resting EKG are inconclusive.

EKGs can be wrong. It is prudent to get a second EKG or other confirmation before pursuing life-threatening treatments. The EKG reading and its interpretation can warn of non-existent danger, while overlooking a real problem.

Stress Electrocardiogram

If doctors can't find anything wrong when they run a resting EKG test, they will often give a Stress EKG. A Stress EKG is very similar to a resting EKG, but with one important difference — the test is conducted with the subject using a treadmill or stationary bicycle. He must pedal or run at a pace set by the doctor. The idea behind a Stress EKG is that abnormalities that don't show up normally can be brought out by putting stress on the cardiovascular system.

Sometimes, the idea works all too well. The exertion of the stress test has been known to induce angina and cause a heart attack. Often, the patient, totally out of shape and possibly ill, is made to exert himself until his cardiovascular system is overstressed. Though the risk of a heart attack is relatively low, it is still very real and unnecessary.

Angiocardiography

The angiogram and angiograph are procedures used to diagnose the condition of the coronary arteries.

In an angiogram, a catheter (a slender tube) is inserted in an artery either in the groin or the arm and threaded into the arteries that feed the heart. On command, the catheter releases dye in the artery to be tested. The dye mixes with the blood, so the cardiologist can watch it on special monitors as it flows through the the artery and into the smaller arterioles. The patient is often moved around so the doctors can look at the arteries from different positions.

Despite the seeming infallibility of the technology, there is substantial room for error by the cardiologist in his interpretation of the the results of the angiogram. The results of an angiogram are usually given to the patient in percentages of blockage that belie the fact that the doctor is only estimating by eyesight, not using a scientific measurement.

As studies have shown, doctors' readings of the same tests can vary widely. Even the same doctor viewing the same test can give a significantly different diagnosis than he gave earlier. Therefore, it is prudent to ask for a second, third, or even fourth opinion of the test. Accuracy is especially important because the next step is usually an angioplasty or coronary bypass.

Despite the fact that an angiogram is considered a "non-invasive" procedure, there is still a risk of complications arising from it. Angiograms have caused angina, heart attacks and strokes. When the catheter is threaded through the maze of arteries on its way to the heart, it can tear or otherwise damage an artery, necessitating an operation to repair it. The catheter can also dislodge material inside the artery, which may resettle in the heart or the brain, triggering a heart attack or stroke.

Before an angiogram, the patient should be tested for allergy to the dye being used in the angiogram. An allergic reaction ocurring on the operating table with a catheter inches from your heart can be disasterous.

Again, the chances of these complications occurring are relatively small, but not so small that a person should be lulled into a false sense of security. Most important, an angiogram puts the patient on the 'fast track' to a more serious angioplasty or a bypass — procedures which entail much greater risks.

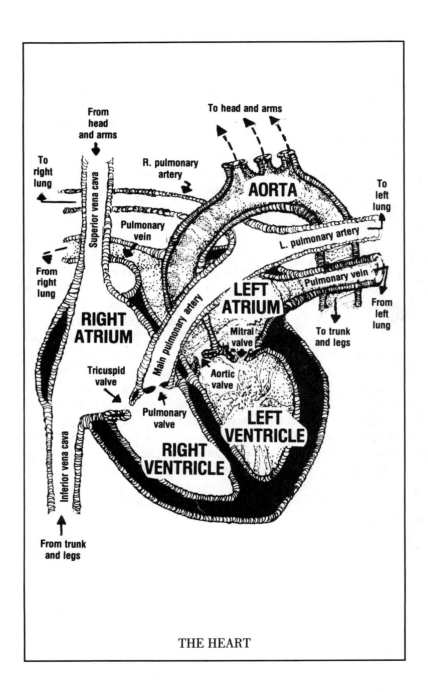

From head and arms

To right lung

R. pulmonary artery

To head and arms

AORTA

To left lung

Superior vena cava

Pulmonary vein

L. pulmonary artery

From right lung

Pulmonary vein

LEFT ATRIUM

From left lung

RIGHT ATRIUM

Main pulmonary artery

Mitral valve

To trunk and legs

Tricuspid valve

Aortic valve

Pulmonary valve

LEFT VENTRICLE

Inferior vena cava

RIGHT VENTRICLE

From trunk and legs

THE HEART

20
SURGERY

"Cure the disease, kill the patient."
—Francis Bacon

Treatments of Heart Disease

Heart disease and its related maladies have been around probably as long as the human race. Over the years, people have tried many treatments (most of them rather painful) to cure it. Many dubious treatments have been based on mistaken ideas of how the body works. They came into use, flourished for a while, then were discredited and disappeared. Despite the vast array of knowledge and stunning technical advances of recent years, we are still locked into a cycle of dubious treatments.

Recent medical history provides many good examples of our folly.

In the late fifties, there was a very popular treatment started by Dr. Claude S. Beck who told of 98% success rates. The treatment? He would open the chest cavity, remove the outer layer of the heart muscle and abraid the heart with asbestos until it was bloody. His reasoning was: in healing the abrassions, the heart would 'grow' more arteries to replace those that were clogged. Eventually, the Beck treatment was discredited and abandoned.

The internal mammary artery bypass operation was even

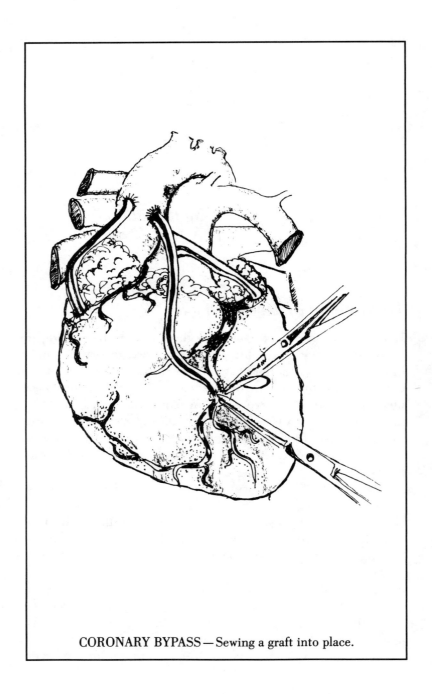

CORONARY BYPASS — Sewing a graft into place.

more popular and distressingly similar to current coronary bypass procedures. It was highly touted by its creator Dr. Arthur S. Vineberg, who told of miraculous recoveries. The operation entailed cutting the mammary arteries, boring a hole into the heart muscle and inserting the mammary arteries. Vineberg thought the heart would "grow" connections to the transplanted arteries.

Finally, in 1972, after 27 years and thousands of patients, Vineberg's operation was at last tested in a double-blind test. His operation failed miserably.

Why are these questionable procedures able to come forth and be unchallenged for so long? The main reason seems to be the medical community's reluctance to challenge them as they are introduced. Invariably, the developer points to a number of people who were miraculously cured as a result of his procedure. It's hard to determine the success of coronary procedures because the symptoms of heart disease are highly subject to the "placebo effect."

If the patient believes the procedure helped him, he will very likely be affected less by the symptoms. He will, in effect, be cured by himself. Therefore, only a 'double-blind' study in which no one knows who got the treatment provides reliable results. Such a study of coronary surgical procedures has never been done. It is interesting to note that the current coronary bypass operation has not been subjected to this test.

Especially today, there is much heated debate over heart disease treatments. Conflicting claims of success and deeply vested interests make the truth hard to identify.

The first thing a doctor is supposed to consider when determining a course of treatment for a patient is whether it will cause more good than harm. The doctor must weigh the negative effects of the treatment against what would happen if the patient were not treated.

Often in these decisions a rather important person is left out of the loop: the patient. Who better knows his body than the patient? Who better know what's important to him? The doctor needs the patient's input.

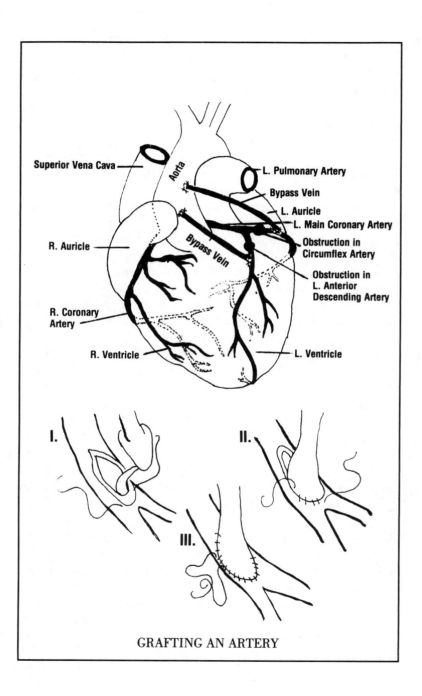

Superior Vena Cava

Aorta

L. Pulmonary Artery

Bypass Vein

L. Auricle

L. Main Coronary Artery

Obstruction in
Circumflex Artery

Obstruction in
L. Anterior
Descending Artery

R. Auricle

Bypass Vein

R. Coronary
Artery

R. Ventricle

L. Ventricle

I.

II.

III.

GRAFTING AN ARTERY

Doctors who don't want the patient involved in this life-and-death decision cannot be trusted to make it themselves.

"Without a doubt, coronary bypass is the most overused operation in the world."
— Dr. Christian Barnard, heart surgeon

Coronary Bypass

The Coronary Bypass is an 'open heart' surgery. That is, surgery done directly on the heart.

THE OPERATION

In a bypass operation, the heart and lungs are stopped, and the blood is circulated and replenished of oxygen by a heart-lung machine. Surgeons take either a vein from the patient's leg or the mammary artery and splice the new vein or artery between the blocked coronary artery and the aorta.

A coronary bypass operation is one of the most difficult operations performed regularly. The difference between success and failure in an operation can depend on one stitch. A stitch that is made one millimeter too deep could close off the artery, leaving the patient in worse shape than before the operation.

Mortality rates from coronary bypass can vary widely from one hospital to the next — even one surgeon to the next. A relatively good mortality rate would be around 2-3%. Bad rates can soar as high as 20%. Mortality rates vary because of caseload. Certain hospitals, especially research and state hospitals, often get patients rejected as bad risks from other hospitals. This usually increases the death rate of 3-4%. A hospital with a mortality rate approaching 10% or more is best avoided.

DISADVANTAGES

Patients lucky enough to make it through the operation alive (5-6% don't), face a long, hard road to recovery.

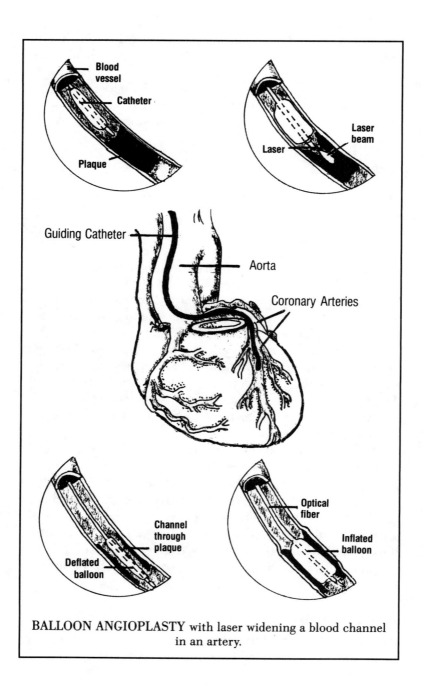

Blood vessel

Catheter

Plaque

Laser beam

Laser

Guiding Catheter

Aorta

Coronary Arteries

Channel through plaque

Deflated balloon

Optical fiber

Inflated balloon

BALLOON ANGIOPLASTY with laser widening a blood channel in an artery.

A coronary bypass operation is a traumatic procedure from which it takes months to recuperate fully. It will be a struggle to sit up, to stand and to walk. Simple tasks will be impossibly difficult, and work, for the first month, is out of the question. The inability to work coupled with the enormous cost ($38,000 in 1989), are not conducive to healing.

Perhaps that is why 20% of people who have a coronary bypass operation undergo significant personality changes including depression, inability to concentrate, forgetfulness and aggressiveness. A more likely theory that could explain this phenomenon is that microscopic bubbles are introduced into the bloodstream by the heart lung machine. The bubbles lodge in the brain, causing subtle but permanent damage.

The transplanted arteries can deteriorate over time, losing their elasticity and hardening like the arteries they replaced. It is not unusual for a patient to require a 're-op'(another bypass operation) three to five years after the first operation. Someone who is experiencing this condition will have the same symptoms (including angina)that they had before their first bypass. Many hospitals won't do a re-op because they consider it to be significantly more risky than a conventional bypass. This is because of the scarring caused by the incisions made in the first operation, and the best arteries or veins were used in the first operation.

Due to the enormous income generated by bypass operations and the tendency of physicians to err on the side of what they consider safety, many people receive bypass operations whose circulatory systems are borderline or well within minimum limits. If fact, studies indicate that at least 44% of bypass operations are unnecessary, subjecting patients to innumerable needless risks including brain damage and often shortening their lives.

Despite the enormous number of coronary bypass operations performed over the past twenty years, there doesn't seem to be a significant advantage to having one. Studies show coronary bypass does not significantly prolong a patient's life compared to others with a similar condition who do not have a bypass. There is also no discernible improvement in the quality of life. Non bypass patients are just as productive as bypass patients.

Angioplasty

The Angioplasty has become more and more popular as an alternative to a Coronary Bypass operation. In 1983, when angioplasties were relatively new, there were 32,000 angioplasties performed in the U.S. By 1988 there were over 200,000 performed, and following current trends, the angioplasty will soon overtake the bypass as the most popular treatment. Why the rapid increase? Perhaps because an angioplasty is a much easier operation to "sell" the patient.

Angioplasties are perceived to be much less risky than bypasses, as they are technically non-invasive and don't involve the use of the dreaded heart-lung machine. The procedure is relatively simple, and the patient is often out of the hospital in days, rather than weeks.

They also cost considerably less: $4,000-5,000 as opposed to $40,000 for a bypass.

Perhaps one of the biggest factors responsible for the rapid increase in the number of angioplasties is the rather warped exposure given them in the media. A recent newspaper article heralding the rise of angioplasty was whimsically titled *The Balloon Man,* and had a soft pastel drawing of a person in surgeon's garb offering multicolored helium balloons to a group of people. The carnival-like atmosphere makes having an angioplasty seem more like a treat than the painful, dangerous treatment it really is.

THE OPERATION

In an Angioplasty, a catheter is inserted in an artery either in the leg or the arm and threaded to the affected artery in the heart. Once there, a balloon on the end of the catheter is inflated in the blocked area, pushing the plaque into the sides of the artery and widening the passage. The catheter is then removed.

Doctors define a "successful" operation as one that widens the arteries by 20% or more leaving the artery with 50% or less blockage.

DISADVANTAGES

The problems associated with Angioplasty primarily concern the treated arteries, which can collapse after treatment, leaving the patient as bad off or worse than before the operation. With approximately 33% of the patients given angioplasties, the treated artery collapses, requiring either another angioplasty or a coronary bypass. The artery may collapse immediately after the operation, or it may collapse up to six months later. Either case may require an emergency bypass operation. 3.5% of angioplasty recipients require an emergency coronary bypass.

There are two ways the artery can collapse:

The damaged area that is dilated by the angioplasty can constrict. This is thought to be caused by either the smooth muscles in the artery reacting to being stretched, or the actual procedure could damage the muscles further, leaving the artery unable to control its own size.

Sometimes the area of the artery downstream from the affected area constricts, necessitating a coronary bypass. The constriction of the artery is thought to be the artery's reaction to the sudden rise in pressure due to the widening of the blocked area.

An angioplasty can also cause damage to unaffected arteries. During placement or removal of the catheter, it can tear or otherwise damage the arteries, necessitating an operation or even a bypass to repair it.

It is important to remember that an angioplasty doesn't remove any of the plaque built up in the artery — it merely pushes it to the sides. The plaque is still there, still catching more material and possibly causing blood clots, which can cause a heart attack or a stroke.

There are new procedures being developed that doctors hope will prevent the collapse of the treated artery.

Artery & Arteriole

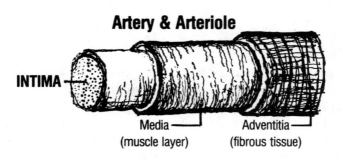

INTIMA

Media
(muscle layer)

Adventitia
(fibrous tissue)

Vein

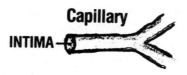

INTIMA

Adventitia
(muscle layer—thin or absent)

Capillary

INTIMA

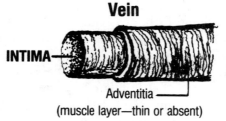

VEIN
(cross section)

ARTERY
(cross section)

Inner
Outer

Outer
Inner
Middle

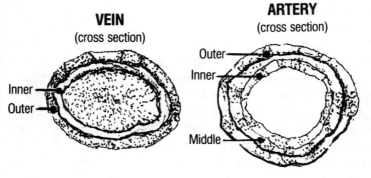

The middle layer is primarily muscular and is used by the body under stress to tighten the blood vessel thus increasing flow of oxygen, etc.

THE STENT

A stent is a piece of wire coiled in the shape of a spring. Stents are often inserted in a clogged artery at the site where a angioplasty has been performed. Once there, it is supposed to keep the artery from collapsing, and smooth out the interior wall, reducing any further deposits and therefore eliminate the need for any further angioplasties in that artery. Unfortunately, in most cases stents have caused problems of their own.

Often the pressure of the stent on the artery inflames the area around it, causing it to become blocked after a short time. More often, despite the use of anti-clotting drugs, a number of blood clots can form, closing the artery. Other times the blood clots that are formed can break off and go to the brain, causing a stroke. It is the opinion of virtually everyone except the stent's most ardent admirers that it does more harm than good.

Alternative Angioplasty Techniques

There are two new variations on the standard Angioplasty. The first is a laser tipped catheter that burns away the fatty deposits and smoothes the sides of the artery. The second technique is to fit the tip of the catheter with a bladed cone. The cone rotates, cutting off plaque and vacuuming it up.

With both of these therapies, it is thought there is less chance of the treated section of the artery closing. Unlike conventional angioplasties, the artery does not undergo the trauma of stretching that occurs when the balloon inflates to clear the plaque deposits in a conventional angioplasty. Though they spare the artery the trauma of stretching, there is still a chance the artery downstream from the affected area may collapse.

The more pressing problem with them is each time the heart beats, the arteries move with it. The abrupt movement makes it extremely difficult for either the laser or the rotating blade to work without cutting into the sides of the artery, or the heart — a dangerous shortcoming.

Because of this, these techniques are still in the experimental stage and will not be widely used for a few years, if ever.

Most important, even when 'successful' all of these therapies described including bypass, only mask the symptoms of arteriosclerosis. Regardless of the jubilant claims of success, they treat a tiny area. There are miles and miles of clogged arteries that are unaffected.

Atherosclerosis is a disease that does not confine itself to the arteries of the heart, but affects the entire circulatory system. Strokes, gangrene, and embolisms are just a few of the conditions that can develop from advanced arterialsclerosis. The effects can be debilitating or fatal.

Often the effectiveness of a coronary bypass or an angiogram is reduced because of the presence of the disease elsewhere in the body. Plaque deposits in other arteries fill in the treated arteries, so they're no clearer than they were before the operation. This may take years, but the effect is serious nonetheless.

It is disheartening that they are still perfecting techniques to clear one or two arteries, when it is really necessary to clear every artery in the body to be free of arterialsclerosis and its hazards.

21
DRUGS

"America has become a nation of junkies."
—Dr. Robert Mendelsohn
Confessions of a Medical Heretic

Well over one billion prescriptions are filled each year by people who have little or no idea what those drugs do, how they do it and the side effects they cause. Their ignorance is reflected in the astronomical number of deaths attributed to prescription drugs each year.

Modern drugs are chemicals. Even if a drug has been derived from an herb, it is so refined, isolated and purified that only a chemical formula remains. That chemical formula is synthesized and mass-produced. Chemicals work on the body much differently than herbs do. Chemicals introduced into the body cause many effects—only some of them are positive. Eli Lilly once said that a drug isn't a drug unless it causes side effects.

Patients taking drugs should know the possible side effects so they are able to recognize them, if they occur.

For Angina

Common forms of *Nitroglycerin*

BRAND NAMES	GENERIC NAMES
Deponit	—
Minitran	—
Nitro-Bid	—
Nitro-Dur	—
Nitrogard	—
Nitroglycerin S.R. (Sustained Release)	—
Nitrol Ointment	—
Nitrolingual Spray	—
Nitrong	—
Nitrostat	—

HOW THEY WORK

Virtually all drugs for angina are forms of Nitroglycerin. Nitroglycerin is quickly absorbed through the skin into the body, usually under the tongue or in any other area where the skin is tender. Though the way Nitroglycerin relieves angina is unclear, it is known to relax the smooth muscles of the arteries, causing them to dilate. This is thought to ease the work the heart must do and enable it to get more blood, relieving the symptoms of angina, though with some people the effectiveness wears off as their condition worsens.

DISADVANTAGES

Extreme care must be taken when handling or storing Nitroglycerin. The same active ingredients that enable it to pass so easily into the body also degrade or evaporate easily, greatly reducing the effectiveness.

Nitroglycerin medication must be stored or carried in a small, airtight (preferably glass) container and kept reasonably cool. Men who carry the medication in their wallets or pockets lose much of the effectiveness through heat loss and fatigued or broken packaging.

Persons who are taking drugs for high blood pressure should be especially careful: the high blood pressure drugs, especially beta-blockers, can lower blood pressure to an unsafe level. When a person who is taking high-blood pressure drugs takes nitroglycerin, his blood pressure can drop so quickly that the brain does not get enough blood for a few moments, causing him to collapse. This can be extremely dangerous, especially for someone who is elderly or driving a car.

For High Blood Pressure

Common forms of *Diuretics (Thiazide)*

BRAND NAMES	GENERIC NAMES
Anhydron	Cyclothiazide
Aquatag	Benzthiazide
Diuril	Chlorothiazide
Enduron	Methyclothiazide
Esidrix	Hydroclorothiazide
Exna	Benzthiazide
Hydrodiuril	Hydrochlorothiazide
Metahydrin	Trichlormethiazide
Naqua	Trichlormethiazide
Naturetin	Bendroflumethiazide
Oretic	Hydrochlorothiazide
Renese	Polythiazide

HOW THEY WORK

Most of the diuretics used to combat high blood pressure are Thiazide diuretics. Diuretics cause the body to shed excess water. This reduction in water reduces the volume of blood, which lessens the load on the circulatory system, lowering the blood pressure.

DISADVANTAGES

The possible side effects of diuretics are serious. Because they tamper with the kidney's natural processes, diuretics put strain on the kidneys and in some cases can cause serious kidney problems. Diuretics can worsen diabeties, cause impotence and ironically, diuretics can also increase cholesterol levels significantly.

Diuretics also cause the body to lose potassium, which may develop into a deficiency. Potassium is vital for many bodily functions, but most importantly the body uses potassium to regulate the electrical system of the heart. Potassium regulates the rhythm of the heart muscles; without potassium, the rhythm of the heart can be disrupted, causing sudden death or other problems. When experiencing a potassium deficiency, dietary supplements should be tried first. Many doctors try to compensate for this side effect by prescribing potassium pills with diuretics, but often the pills have side effects of their own and cannot keep pace.

There are potassium-sparing diuretics available, but they bring with them side effects that are undesireable.

Common forms of *Beta-Blockers*	
BRAND NAMES	**GENERIC NAMES**
Blocadren	Timolol
Corgard	Nadolol
Inderol	Propranolol
Lorpressor	Metoprolol
Normodyne	Labetalol
Sectral	Acebutolol
Tenormin	Atenolol
Trandate	Labetalol
Visken	Pindolol

HOW THEY WORK

Beta-Blockers work by partially suppressing the electronic processes that trigger the beating of the heart, making the heart beat slower and with less force. This smoothing of the heart's beat lowers the peaks of the upper (systolic) blood pressure reading.

DISADVANTAGES

Beta-blockers have many serious side effects. Some of the common ones are: loss of energy, dizziness, fatigue, impotence, worsening of congestive heart disease, elevated cholesterol, depression or nightmares, bronchiospasms (asthma-like attacks) and loss of appetite.

Many of the side effects of Beta-blockers will necessitate dramatic changes in the user's lifestyle. The loss of energy with Beta-blockers can leave a person virtually incapacitated, making the simplest tasks impossible.

Beta-blockers are only appropriate in emergency situations. The drugs' potency and abundance of serious side effects make them of use only to people whose blood pressure is over 200. It is unfortunate that the medical community has shown a total lack of restraint in prescribing them.

The most important thing to consider about any drug or surgical treatment is that the treatment does more good than harm. With regard to these drugs, that does not seem to be the case. In the MR FIT (Multiple Risk Factor Inventory Trial) study, researchers found the mortality rate was significantly higher among subjects whose high blood pressure was treated aggressively with drugs over those who weren't. There is no proof these medications will help you live longer. In fact, they may significantly shorten your life.

Cholesterol Reducers

Common forms of *Cholesterol Reducers*

BRAND NAMES	GENERIC NAMES
Atromid-S	Chlofibrate
Cholybar	Cholestyramine
Colestid Granules	Colestipol
Lopid	Gemfibrozil
Lorelco	Probucol
Mevacor	Lovastatin
Nia-Bid	Niacin
Niacor	Niacin
Nicobid	Niacin
Nicolar	Niacin
Questran	Cholestyramine
S-P-T	—
Slo-Niacin	Niacin

HOW THEY WORK

Most of the commonly prescribed cholesterol lowering medications work by attaching themselves to the bile acids in the intestine. The drugs are indigestible and therefore pass out of the body, taking the bile acids with them. To compensate, the liver makes more bile acids.

Cholesterol is one of the major building blocks of bile acid, so the liver takes the cholesterol necessary to make it from the blood stream, thereby lowering the amount of cholesterol in the blood.

DISADVANTAGES

There are numerous side effects attributed to these drugs including constipation, gas, heartburn and bloating. In one clinical test with Cholestyramine, the CPPT, the percentage of people who suffered moderate to severe side effects was an overwhelming sixty-eight percent.

Other more serious conditions that have been attributed to the drug are impairment of liver function, increased risk of gallstones and cancer. The dangers of having low cholesterol are another matter entirely.

Cholesterol is one of the major components in the body and is used by the body for the manufacture of steroids, sex hormones and is a major component of the brain. These points are especially significant when considering the rise in accidental and violent deaths experienced by the subjects of the CPPT study.

The number of accidental or violent deaths more than doubled in the group taking cholesterol-lowering drugs over the control group. Whether this is due to the chemical changes in the body or is a fluke, the biggest surprise is the total number of deaths in each group. In a study in which 1906 people were given Cholestyramine daily for 7.4 years, there were only three fewer heart attack deaths than in the control group, which took no drugs.

There is no definitive proof that lowering your cholesterol with Cholestyramine will help you live longer. While there were fewer deaths due to heart attack in the group taking the drug, the deaths due to other health problems negate any gain.

Blood Thinners

Common forms of *Blood Thinners*	
BRAND NAMES	**GENERIC NAMES**
Anacin	Aspirin
Bufferin	—
Easprin	—
Empirin	—
Excedrin	—
Florinal	—
Gelpirin	—

Common forms of *Blood Thinners (cont'd)*

BRAND NAMES	GENERIC NAMES
Lortab	—
Norgesic	—
Percodan	—
Soma Compound	—
Supac	—
Talwin	—
Zorprin	—

HOW THEY WORK:

Acetylsalicylic Acid, the chemical name for aspirin, has been around since the early 1800's, but the substance that aspirin was derived from has been around for over 1,000 years. It was the Chinese who first popularized the use of willow bark for pain-relieving purposes. In the 1800's, various derivatives of the bark were tested until the form of aspirin that we now use was settled on.

Even though aspirin has been around for almost 200 years, we still don't understand fully how it works. Aspirin is thought to interfere with the body's production of a series of chemicals called prostaglandins. Prostaglandins regulate many of the body's functions. Aspirin is widely used for two of them: body temperature and pain. Aspirin's effect on the blood-clotting process is less well known. Prostaglandins are also very important in the body's blood-clotting process. By interfering with the prostaglandins, aspirin reduces the blood's tendency to form clots. People who have a history of heart disease or stroke generally have blood that clots too easily. It is thought that aspirin can decrease the likelihood of clots forming, which can trigger a stroke or heart attack.

All forms of aspirin, whether a $5.00 bottle of Extra-Strength Bufferin or an $.89 no-name brand, have the same chemical composition and are equally effective. They only differ in form (capsules, gum, tablets) and the extra ingredients such as flavors and buffering agents.

DISADVANTAGES

Because aspirin has been around for years, and is so widely used, many people don't even consider it a drug, much less a dangerous one. However, it is well known that aspirin can cause serious and almost fatal bleeding problems. It is the most common cause of fatal drug overdoses in children. Many of these incidents occur because the people using or administering the drug don't take it seriously. This can be a fatal error.

One misconception when taking aspirin for heart disease is to assume that the higher dose that is taken, the more effective it will be. It is only necessary to take 40 mg. to achieve the anti-clotting effect. Any more is dangerous overkill. Most forms of aspirin have much more than 40 mg. of the drug. Children's aspirin usually has at least 80 mg!

An overdose of aspirin can have many harmful effects and can even be fatal. Overdosing can cause excessive bleeding in the stomach or the brain. Aspirin is well known as a stomach irritant, and overuse or use by people who are susceptible can cause severe irritation or bleeding.

People who are highly sensitive to aspirin should refrain from taking it if the risks outweigh the benefits. People who experience some stomach irritation from aspirin may be able to get by with buffered or coated aspirin. Keep in mind, however, using aspirin for heart disease is a long-term proposition. It is much harder for the stomach to withstand long-term irritation than occasional irritation.

Other forms of pain-killing drugs such as Tylenol (Acetaminophen) and Advil (Ibuprofen) are useless against heart disease. They have no anti-clotting effect on the blood, and do nothing to defend against heart attacks or strokes. Make sure that whatever product you use contains aspirin. It is not enough that it is a pain-reliever.

General heart aids

Common forms of *Digitalis*

BRAND NAMES	GENERIC NAMES
Cedilanid-D	Deslanoside
Crystodigin	Digitoxin
Lanoxin	Digoxin

HOW THEY WORK

This drug is derived from Fox Glove, a toxic plant. Digitalis is called a glycoside, that is, it stimulates the heart muscle's ability to turn chemical energy in to mechanical energy. This strengthens the heart muscles, enabling them to beat more forcefully.

DISADVANTAGES

Toxicity is a significant problem with digitalis. Overdose, intoxication and adverse reactions to the drug can often cause death. These situations are so serious and common that there is an emergency drug, Digibind, which has been formulated to bind with digitalis and take it out of the body. Unfortunately the drug may not work quickly enough to save the victim.

Early symptoms of overdose are nausea, vomiting and diarrhea. In the later stages headaches, weakness and apathy with increasingly worse arrithmias can possibly lead to death.

Digitalis, even when administered properly, often has disruptive effects on the heart's beating cycle, causing the heart to beat irregularly. Digitalis significantly increases the risk of sudden death in people who have survived a heart attack. Digitalis is especially dangerous with people who are taking diuretics. Low potassium causes the heart muscle to become sensitive to digitalis, causing an overdose even with normal doseage. Calcium loss must also be watched for the same reasons, as calcium is also vital for proper heart function.

TERMS OF HEART DISEASE

by Colin Quinn

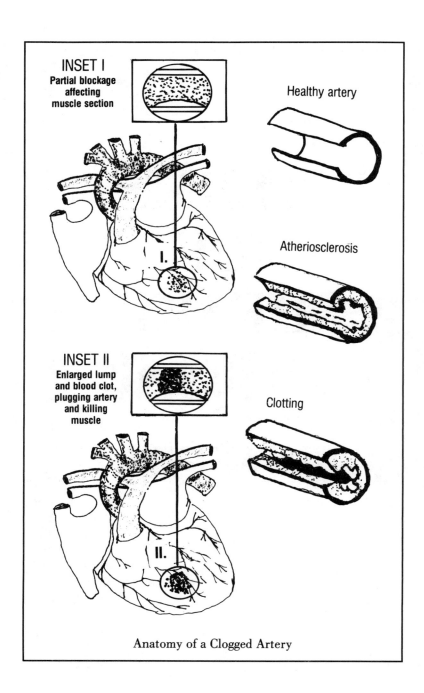

INSET I
Partial blockage affecting muscle section

Healthy artery

I.

Atheriosclerosis

INSET II
Enlarged lump and blood clot, plugging artery and killing muscle

Clotting

II.

Anatomy of a Clogged Artery

Arteriosclerosis

Artertiosclerosis is a thickening and hardening of the arteries. It often takes place in the coronary arteries that feed the heart.

The human artery has three layers: an outer arterial wall, a middle layer of smooth muscle cells and an inner (endothelial) layer.

No one is sure what causes Arteriosclerosis, though it is thought the process begins with damage or irritation to the middle layer of the artery. The irritation can be caused by smoking, cholesterol, free radicals or high blood pressure. Some researchers think a virus may irritate the artery and cause artertialsclerosis.

The body attempts to heal the injury by making more smooth muscle cells. This causes the arterial wall to bulge inward. The bulge acts as a snag, accumulating cholesterol, fatty deposits and dead cell tissue. The deposited material is called plaque. Eventually, the plaque build-up may make the artery so narrow, a blood clot or other obstruction can plug it completely, cutting off the blood supply and causing a heart attack.

Angina

Angina occurs when the heart, because of narrowed arteries or some other circulatory problem, doesn't get enough oxygen. Angina pain is the heart's way of warning us before real damage occurs.

Angina is characterized by pain starting from the center of the chest and spreading to the shoulders and down the insides of the arms. Often, there is a pinching or heavy sensation in the center of the chest, making it difficult to breathe. The symptoms of angina are often confused with other problems, such as indigestion. Pain in the chest can have many causes.

When someone suspects he has angina pain, he should lie down with his head and shoulders raised to relieve the heart of stress, enabling it to replenish itself. If the pain does go away after resting, it is further evidence of angina.

Heart Attack

Virtually all heart attacks occur when a narrowed coronary artery is closed by a blood clot, cutting off blood to the area fed by the clogged artery. Without a supply of blood, the heart muscle can die. After some heart attacks, the heart learns to compensate for the lost muscle, becoming almost as efficient as it was before. With more massive heart attacks, disability or death often results.

A heart attack is signaled by moderate to severe angina, which isn't relieved by rest. The pain is often accompanied by sweating, dizziness, nausea and unconsciousness.

The most dangerous part of a heart attack occurs when the heart misfires. This misfiring can be due either to mechanical or electrical failure.

In a mechanical failure, a significant portion of the heart muscle is deprived of oxygen and begins to die. The other muscles of the heart must learn to compensate for the dying area. The severity of a heart attack depends on how large an area dies and how hard it is for the rest of the heart to compensate. Sometimes, such a large or vital part of the muscle dies that the rest of the heart cannot compensate. The result is death.

An electrical failure is more complicated. The interaction of the heart muscles is complex and exacting. The heart is essentially a two-stage pump. The blood is drawn into the atrium, which contracts, pumping it into the ventricle. Then the ventricle contracts, sending the blood out into the body.

The contractions of the ventricles and the atriums must be precisely synchronized for the heart to work right. The muscles of the heart are electronically controlled to ensure synchronization. Certain muscles relay the electronic signal to other muscles. When these relay muscles are damaged in a heart attack, the signal is disrupted, so the heart may not be able to start pumping again.

RISK FACTORS OF HEART DISEASE

by Colin Quinn

"You make the health decisions because you're doing the dying, and when you die, you die alone."

R.F. Quinn

No one knows the exact cause of heart disease, although certain risk factors have been identified. The connection between risk factors and an actual heart attack is much more nebulous than you may think.

Risk factors are based entirely on statistics. Certain characteristics are shared by people who have heart disease. These characteristics are called risk factors. While this may seem an ideal way to predict future heart trouble, the statistical evidence is often inconsistent. Statistics can't tell us if a given person will get heart disease. They only indicate risk.

Even if a person is 'at risk' for all the factors listed below, there is no guarantee he will develop heart disease. Conversely, even if a person has no risk factors, he may get a heart attack.

A diabetic, obese smoker with high blood pressure could quite possibly live well into his nineties, while a trim, healthy person may have a fatal heart attack at 42, like Jim Fixx, the fitness guru. He pioneered the fitness craze with his book called *Running*, only to die of a heart attack while jogging. While risk factors may suggest the likelihood of heart disease, only time will tell.

High Blood Pressure

The human heart is a pump. Like most pumps, the heart needs to exert a certain amount of force to push your blood through your circulatory system. The force (or pressure) required to circulate blood through the body is different for each individual, and depends on a number of factors, many of which aren't fully understood. The main obstacle the heart has to work against are the arterioles. The arterioles restrict the blood flow, forcing it through the capillaries, some of which are so small that blood cells can only move through them one cell at a time.

A person is considered to have high blood pressure when the force his heart has to exert to circulate blood is higher than that considered "normal" or "healthy."

Normal, Borderline and High are arbitrary categories based on statistical norms. They do not mean a person is healthy or unhealthy, but only suggest a degree of risk.

It is important to take blood pressure reading repeatedly over a period of time. Blood pressure can vary widely due to both physical and psychological factors such as illness and stress. So many things affect blood pressure, it is not often known what causes it to be high.

For example, it could be due to obesity or smoking, the stress of a long day at work or the forty-five minute wait in the doctor's office. Of patients diagnosed with high blood pressure, doctors are able to determine the cause in only 10% of the cases.

An example of the continuing medical mystery surrounding blood pressure is a recent study which said what we've been hearing for years is wrong. The study showed salt intake has no significant influence on blood pressure for most people.

Doctors know the actual cause of only 10% of high blood pressure, but they can control 90% of it. Diet and exercise can effectively control blood pressure, but it is usually done artificially with drugs.

While high blood pressure may not cause death, it often aggravates existing problems, increasing the risk of heart attack or stroke. It is also thought to cause arteriosclerosis by injuring the inner walls of arteries because of the stress it puts on them.

Stress and Lifestyle

Stress can be a contributing factor to the development of arteriosclerosis. In response to stress, the muscles of the arteries constrict, raising blood pressure and making the heart work harder to keep up. Narrowing of the arteries can be especially dangerous in arteries that are already partially blocked by arteriosclerosis, taking them one step closer to being totally blocked by a blood clot.

People who are "run-down" have less resistance to illness — including arteriosclerosis. Fitness keeps the circulatory system in good shape, making it more resistant to arteriosclerosis and more able to recover from any trauma that might occur.

Smoking

Again, smoking is not a cause of arteriosclerosis by itself, but it is a well-established contributing factor. Smoking is thought to cause the formation of 'free radicals', which are irritants that can attack the walls of the arteries. Free radicals are found in tobacco smoke and other common irritants. They cause lesions in the arteries that provide the foundation for arterial deposits of minerals, cholesterol and other debris.

Smoking also affects the circulatory system adversely because of the added stress it places on it. The carbon monoxide in cigarette smoke attaches itself to blood cells, so they can't carry oxygen to the heart and other parts of the body. Smoking also causes the arteries to constrict, reducing even further their ability to circulate blood. In a circulatory system already hampered by arteriosclerosis, smoking can push it beyond its capacity to meet the body's needs, causing angina or worsening a heart attack.

Diet and Cholesterol

There has been much said about the effect of cholesterol on the body's cardiovascular system. Supermarkets are awash in products that loudly proclaim their lack of cholesterol. Pamphlets from the American Heart Association and other medical organizations list the reduction of cholesterol intake as one of their primary recommendations for avoiding heart disease. The medical profession and food industry have made cholesterol to appear almost poisonous, when it is actually essential for life. Cholesterol is needed for many of the body's crucial processes. Without it, we would surely die.

The human body is a complex factory, capable of synthesizing many different substances. One of those substances is cholesterol. Cholesterol is present in every cell in the body.

There are actually two forms of cholesterol: HDL (high density lipoprotein), and LDL (low density lipoprotein). The level of LDL in the body is controlled by the liver, which makes both LDL and HDL. The body also gets LDL from the food it digests. HDL goes into the body and attaches itself to an LDL molecule, which it back carries to the liver, effectively taking it the out of body. If the liver determines there too is much LDL in the body, it will manufacture more HDL. Likewise, if there is too little LDL, it will reduce the amount of HDL and manufacture more LDL. That's how the liver controls the level of cholesterol in the body.

There is absolutely no evidence to prove that lowering your cholesterol will enable you to live longer. Numerous tests (LRC-CPPT, MR. FIT, Heart-Diet Pilot) have failed to show that reduction of cholesterol through drugs or diet will result in a longer life.

The body regulates its own blood cholesterol level through an elaborate and complex system. Attempts to tamper with this system may reduce blood cholesterol but can also upset the body's natural balance, causing a series of problems much more hazardous than high cholesterol.

The death rate for people who manage their cholesterol with drugs and those who don't is virtually identical. While heart attack rate may diminish slightly when cholesterol is lowered, the maladies caused by cholesterol lowering drugs negate any gain.

Unlike what we have been told, cholesterol level is only important to certain segments of the population. Medical studies show that cholesterol levels are a related to heart disease only among men age 35 to 50 and women between 40 and 50. There was no correlation between high cholesterol and the incidence of heart disease among the elderly. Women are not usually at risk for heart disease until they reach menopause, so they effectively skip the period when cholesterol might matter.

Because the amount of cholesterol present in the body is regulated by the body itself, changes in the intake of dietary cholesterol are largely insignificant. Radical changes in diet, from a diet high in cholesterol to one totally devoid of cholesterol only decrease a person's blood cholesterol level by 10 percent at most.

Since they interfere with the body's natural processes, cholesterol lowering drugs can cause a host of serious side effects and must be taken for the rest of one's life. They are discussed further in the section on drugs.

Considering the huge effort and considerable risk of lowering cholesterol, and the very limited benefit, if any, it is curious the medical profession has focused its energies so forcefully on it. Perhaps its because cholesterol control has become a $20 billion-a-year business for the drug companies and medical establishment.

Heredity

Heredity is very important. It influences the blood pressure, cholesterol and other traits that determine a one's resistant to arteriosclerosis.

Just as we inherit facial features from our parents, we inherit traits that make us resistant or susceptible to arteriosclerosis. The way the body metabolizes cholesterol and the tendency of arteries to become inflamed are two of many inherited traits.

There is no way of knowing which traits you have inherited. Even if both sides of the family have a history of heart disease, you may not inherit those traits. But it does indicate statistical degree of risk.

"A healthy population means a dead pharmaceutical industry."

Hans Reesch, *Naked Express*

BIBLIOGRAPHY

Books About Conventional Medicine

Drugs, Drugs and More Drugs, Dr. Kurt W. Donsbach
Internat'l Institute of Natural Health Sciences
Huntington Beach, California 92646

Physicians' Desk Reference, 1991 edition
Medical Economics, Inc., Oradell, New Jersey 07649

Medicine on Trial, by Inlander, Levin and Weiner
Pantheon Books, New York

What Your Doctor Didn't Learn in Medical School
by Stuart M. Berger, M.D.
Wm. Morrow Co., New York

Heart Bypass by Gloria Hochman.
Ballantine Books, New York

Heart Myths by Bruce D. Charash, M.D.
Viking Press, New York

Heart Failure by Thomas J. Moore
Touchstone Books, New York

Drug Information for the Consumer, Consumers Union
Mount Vernon, New York

Bypassing Bypass by Arline Brecher and Elmer Cranton, M.D.
Stein & Day, Briarcliff Manor, New York

Taber's Cyclopedic Medical Dictionary, 12th edition.
Clayton L. Thomas M.D., ed. 12th edition
F.A. Davis Co., Philadelphia

Confessions of a Medical Heretic by Dr. Robert S. Mendelsohn
Contemporary Books, Chicago

Prescription Drugs by the editors of Consumer Guide
Publications International, Lincolnwood, Ilinois

Worst Pills/Best Pills by the Public Citizen Health Research Group
Washington D.C.

Pills, Profits and Politics by Silverman and Lee
University of California Press, Los Angeles

Pills That Don't Work by Coley and Wolfe
Public Citizen Health Research Group, New York

Medical Overkill by Ralph C. Greene, M.D.
Geo. Stickley Co., Philadelphia

Drugs from A to Z by Richard R. Lingeman
McGraw Hill, New York

Heartbook: Guide by the American Heart Assn.
E.P. Dutton, New York

Medicine on Trial by Dannie Abse
Crown Publishers, New York

Heart Attack by Donsbach and Nittler
Institute of Natural Health Sciences, Huntington Beach, California

Books on Herbs and Alternative Medicine

Scientific Validation of Herbal Medicine by Dan Mowrey, PhD.
Cormorant Books, Lehi, Utah

Cayenne by Dan Mowrey, PhD.
Cormorant Books, Lehi, Utah.

Next Generation Herbal Medicine by Dan Mowrey, Phd.
Keats Publishing, New Canaan, Connecticut

Century Book of Health, 1906.
King-Richardson Co., Chicago

The Way of Herbs by Michael Tierra
Washington Square Press, New York

Nutritional Herbology by Mark Pedersen
Pedersen Publishing, Bountiful, Utah

Dictionary of Modern Herbalism by Simon Sims
Healing Arts Press, Rochester, Vermont

Herbal Medications by David G. Spoerke, Jr.
Woodbridge Press, Santa Barbara, California

21st Century Herbal by Dr. Michael Murray
Vita Line, Bellevue, Washington

Culpeper's Herbal Remedies by Dr. Nicholas Culpeper
Wilshire Books, No. Hollywood, California

Weiner's Herbal by Michael Weiner, PhD.
Quantum Books, Mill Valley, California

Prescription for Nutritional Healing by James and Phyllis Balch
Avery Publishing, Garden City Park, New York

Herbal Medicine by Dian Dincin Buchman
Gramercy Publishing, New York

Herbal Home Health Care by Dr. John Christopher
Christopher Pub., Springville, Utah

School of Natural Healing by Dr. John Christopher
Christopher Pub., Springville, Utah

Capsicum by Dr. John Christopher
Christopher Pub., Springville, Utah

Rodale's Encyclopedia of Herbs
Rodale Press, Emmaus, Pennsylvania

Nature's Medicines by Richard Lucas
Parker Pub., West Nyack, New York

The Magic of Herbs by Richard Lucas
Parker Pub., West Nyeack, New York

Miracle Medicine Herbs by Richard Lucas
Parker Pub., West Nyack, New York

The Herb Book by Boxer and Back
Peerage Books, London

Science of Herbal Medicine by John Heinerman
Bi-World Pub., Orem, Utah

Holistic Health Handbook of the Berkeley Holistic Health Center
Berkeley, California

The Herb Book by John Lust
Bantam Books, New York

The Herbal Handbook by David Hoffman
Healing Arts Press, Rochester, Vermont

Back to Eden by Jethro Kloss
Back to Eden Books, Loma Linda, California

Herbs & Things by Jeanne Rose
Grosset & Dunlap, New York

The Vitamin Herb Guide
Global Health, Alberta, Canada

Herbally Yours by Penny C. Royal
Sound Nutrition, Payson, Utah.

Natural Healing with Herbs by Humbart Santillo
Hohm Press, Prescott, Arizona

Herbal Pharmacist by Linda Rector-Page.

Modern Herbal by Mrs. M. Grieve
Dover Pub., New York

Nature's Remedies by Joseph E. Meyer
Indiana Botanic Gardens, Hammond, Indiana

Heart Nutrition by Richard R. Keene, M.D.
Wellness International, Fort Worth, Texas

Health and Healing by Andrew Weil, M.D.
Houghton Miflin Co., Boston, Massachusetts

High Blood Pressure by Dr. Kurt Donsbach

Peppers by Jean Andrews
University of Texas Press, Austin, Texas

The Whole Chile Pepper Book by DeWitt and Gerlach.
Little, Brown & Co., Canada

Dictionary of Natural Health by Nevill & Susan Drury
Sterling Publishing, New York

Information was also gathered from the *Herbalgram*, the *Herb Companion*, the *NY Times*, the *Minneapolis Tribune* and many other periodicals.

INDEX